ONE SIGNAL
PUBLISHERS

ATRIA

EVERY MOMENT IS A LIFE

Gaza in the Time of Genocide

Compiled by
susan abulhawa

Editors
susan abulhawa | English
Huzama Habayeb | Arabic

Translators
susan abulhawa
Kay Heikkinen

A Collaboration Project Between
Palestine Writes and the Culture and Free Thought Association

ONE SIGNAL
PUBLISHERS

ATRIA

NEW YORK AMSTERDAM/ANTWERP LONDON
TORONTO SYDNEY/MELBOURNE NEW DELHI

ATRIA
An Imprint of Simon & Schuster, LLC
1230 Avenue of the Americas
New York, NY 10020

First One Signal Publishers/Atria Paperback edition February 2026

ONE SIGNAL PUBLISHERS/ATRIA PAPERBACK and colophon are registered trademarks of Simon & Schuster, LLC

Simon & Schuster strongly believes in freedom of expression and stands against censorship in all its forms. For more information, visit BooksBelong.com.

For information about special discounts for bulk purchases, please contact Simon & Schuster Special Sales at 1-866-506-1949 or business@simonandschuster.com.

The Simon & Schuster Speakers Bureau can bring authors to your live event. For more information or to book an event, contact the Simon & Schuster Speakers Bureau at 1-866-248-3049 or visit our website at www.simonspeakers.com.

Interior design by Kyoko Watanabe

Manufactured in the United States of America

3 5 7 9 10 8 6 4 2

Library of Congress Cataloging-in-Publication Data has been applied for.

ISBN 978-1-6682-2236-2 (pbk)
ISBN 978-1-6682-2237-9 (ebook)

Contents

EVERY MOMENT IS A LIFE

Introduction
by susan abulhawa

Many of us knew on October 8, 2023, that Israel was going to unleash the full deadly power of its military might on the Palestinian people. In many circles of Israeli society—be they political, economic, academic, or social—there had been growing calls to "kill them all," long before the seven decades-long Indigenous resistance movement led to the operation on October 7, 2023.

All of us—the diaspora and people of conscience—scrambled to find a way to get aid into Gaza. It was nearly impossible. But after failed attempts, I found myself on the other side of impossible, in Gaza—dear Gaza, Palestine—in February 2024. Through Playgrounds for Palestine, we brought aid and implemented local projects for children. Then I went back again a month later.

Witness, coffee, and Indigenous healing circles

I will not repeat here what I have written and spoken about extensively, except to say that, in Egypt, I bore witness to what can only be described as a theater of aid—performance from at least one organization taking money without accountability and sending into Gaza truckloads of boxes that were mostly empty.

When I was able to enter myself—in February 2024, then again in April 2024—I took as many bags as I could carry: over 20 on the first trip and 40 on the second. It was a drop in the ocean of need, but significant for those who received it. The most popular item among hospital staff and friends was coffee. I had packed about 20 pounds of it, which afforded me instant popularity. The simple dignity of having a cup of brew in the morning had been denied to most people in Gaza.

They had been robbed of everything—everything, except their dignity, faith, and humanity. I often felt small in their presence, repeatedly humbled by the hospitality, kindness, and generosity of people who had so little to give, but gave nonetheless. When I left Gaza the first time (and again the second time), I had received enough gifts to fill a small bag—handmade keychains, a knitted hat, a beaded bracelet, embroidered cloth, drawings.

Of course, I collected as many stories while there as I could. Most were obtained from women recovering in the hospital. Frequently, their stories contained information they'd learned after the fact, and they narrated them with detachment, until I probed. What did it sound like? How did it smell? Feel? What was your first thought?

They let me ask, and they were generous in their answers. That's when the tears fell, and all the women around them gave their support and love. They all told me that those evenings together were the first time any of them had explored the sensory details of their trauma, much less uttered them.

What was meant to be a gathering of testimonies ended up being a kind of Indigenous therapy—this world of Palestinian women who spoke to each other of their darkest, most terrifying moments in the midst of an ongoing genocide. This is how our foremothers healed their wounds, in the emotional safety of other women who received their words tenderly and cradled them in understanding, who gave comfort and love to one another.

Ultimately, I found another way to be of service.

Majeda and Maha, and CFTA

Although I was mostly confined to a medical facility on that first trip, I did manage to move about on my own a few times. My dear friends Majeda Saqqa and Maha elRa'ee asked if I would hold a writing workshop for some of the young people at the Culture and Free Thought Association (CFTA). It was an easy yes, and we managed to have two sessions before I had to leave the first time. But during my second trip, less than a month later, I had more freedom to move about and made the workshops a priority.

Majeda and her entire family had been displaced from their grand historic family home in Khan Younis, and Maha elRa'ee and her family had taken them all into theirs in Rafah. I had the privilege of staying with them a couple of nights, all of us sleeping on the floor in rows. They shared their food with me, and once even insisted I accept bathwater, which they heated for me on an outdoor hearth. It was humbling to be in their presence, to be surrounded by such generosity from people who had so little left in the world. Such openness, sharing, and instant family was emblematic of Palestinian society in Gaza during a veritable genocide.

Israel eventually bombed Maha's home, reducing that house of love to rubble, and everyone was forced to seek refuge elsewhere. Thankfully, they survived.

Emergence of this anthology

All of the young writers included in this collection had also been displaced from their homes. All of them had lost loved ones to Israel's relentless violence. All had seen, heard, and felt the unfathomable. The first couple of hours of our first workshop were spent doing writing exercises. On the surface, I wanted to get a sense of their writing styles and literary sense. But the more important aim of those exercises was for us to get to know each other and create an atmosphere of trust.

I had never met any of them before that first workshop. They ranged in age from early twenties to mid-thirties. It was clear from those early writing exercises that some possessed real talent and could indeed write first-rate narratives.

That was when I realized that perhaps the most important contribution I could make in this genocide would be to impart whatever skills I had to empower emerging writers.

Palestinians in Gaza should be given every platform to narrate this extraordinary moment in history, the terrible details of which only they can truly know.

Thus, the idea for this anthology was born.

The workshops

The workshops were held on the beach and in the courtyard of CFTA's office, under the constant buzzing of zanana drones and the frequent sounds of distant bombs. Some of the writers traveled for two hours to get there, not because the distance was far, but because of the limited pace with which one could move about in the densely packed region of Mawasi Khan Younis after Israel pushed nearly all of Gaza's northern population there. Whether the writers traveled on a donkey cart, in a car, or on a bicycle, 5 to 15 miles per hour was the best they could manage.

After the writing exercises, I asked each of them to pen a story, poem, song, memoir, or any other short or long-form piece. The next time we met, they'd go around one at a time, reading what they wrote, followed by feedback from the others and from myself. Each session was like that, with discussions about styles of writing, literary devices, plot, and various aspects of effective storytelling.

Some of the early drafts were written like reports of their lives, so the thing we worked on the most was making the story "smaller," to hone in on the sensory details, from which the larger story of genocide would emerge without stating it explicitly. The transformation was remarkable. As they began to focus on the minutiae—the scent of bread baking in the morning, the feel of dust on their skin and the ringing silence in their ears after an explosion, the melody of their mother's voice calling them home—their stories took on a vivid, palpable quality. The narratives became not just accounts of events but immersive experiences, drawing the reader into the heart of their reality.

I watched as their confidence grew with each session, their voices becoming stronger, clearer, more assured. There was a sense of camaraderie and mutual respect among them. Several broke down in tears reading their own words, sometimes hearing the details spoken aloud for the first time. We teared with them. These writers were not only refining their craft, but also locating power in their stories as Indigenous sons and daughters of the land in a time of colonial genocide.

The writers, the love

Maher Daoud—Abu Mahmoud—at CFTA organized and managed each session, diligently communicating with the writers and getting them to and from the meeting location. He read over the stories and selected the final contributors, copyediting an earlier iteration of the manuscript. Like every writer in this anthology, he took great risks to get to the meetings and tried to capture moments of normalcy in an utterly abnormal time, without his wife and child, without reliable electricity to charge his phone, without the security of food and water and shelter.

Each of the writers carried extraordinary trauma, evident in their eyes and bodies. I fell in love with them all, and I feel changed by them. Amrou Al-Najar usually opened or closed our sessions, singing in his soulful voice. The genocide had transformed his orderly life into chaos, and he spent his days trying to assemble pieces that no longer fit, like trying to manage a cup of coffee in the morning, a decadent luxury item in his new life.

Diana Islayh was usually quiet, even when she read, her voice barely audible beneath the awful buzz of Israeli drones. She said something to me in passing that stuck in my mind. "My life does not resemble me," she said. "It's terrifying that I've adjusted to it . . . like I'm becoming someone else." The early version of Diana's story was fully formed and moved us all. Maram Hammou was likewise soft-spoken. The anguish of losing her aunt cracked her voice with every reading. She is a third-year medical student who saw her entire university vanish overnight, leaving her lost and bewildered. She seemed to grasp at any thread of hope, anything that resembled the encouragement of her beloved aunt.

Reema Abu Mousa remained guarded. Anger and frustration, rather than anguish, were more evident in her. Everyone would nod in comprehension when she read her piece to the group. While I can imagine the pain in their lives, I know I can never fully understand. But I could certainly relate to the blessing of anger. Samya Al-Laham and her cousin Saja Laham embarked on this writing journey together. Each of them experimented with multiple stories, all of them moving through extraordinary loss. It was rewarding to watch their process of sifting through so many big events, before settling finally on singular moments. For Samya, it was a brief, but profound encounter with an elder in the street who mended her shoe. Saja committed to paper the instant her life pivoted from home to homelessness. I watched them confer with each other through their eyes, a lovely and gentle handholding among kin.

Fatma Asfour was always the best dressed among us all. Even in the deprivation of those impossible months, she was all about style. Her clothes, hair, and shoes were as meticulous as the circumstances allowed. She walked like a model, head always high, shoulders back. She had made a daring journey on bicycle, risking it all to rescue her clothes, and made no apology for it. Unlike others, Khuloud Abu Zaher didn't wear her pain. It was there, surely, behind a bold and confident insistence on work and production. She arrived prepared, did all the homework, and had no time to waste on tears, at least not in the workshops. She listened intently to everyone's critique and was direct and honest in her assessment of the work of others. Her presence was authentic and powerful.

Rizq Ahmad was a gentle soul with an abiding sense of family. It was clear from his writing and the way he spoke that he was fortified with strong and intimate family bonds. While that is somewhat typical in Palestinian families, it felt especially warm in his case. He could survive, even find merriment and joy living in a tent with meager international aid, after having lived a well-off existence, as long as they were together. His piece tells me just that.

Lubna Meqdad was in search of a happy ending, some silver lining to what was unfathomable. Her experience of quite literally dodging bombs, moving from one tent to another, and surviving on food they'd never consume in normal times were harrowing (though common for all Palestinians in Gaza). But she would end nearly everything she said with a hopeful sentiment, like a punctuation mark that cannot bear or believe the sentence before it. Her tentative but sure smile was an embodiment of the search for the proverbial light at the end of the tunnel. Maysa Salama was that way too, insisting that the end of their stories in life and on paper would close with the triumph of defiance that baffles all colonizers throughout time. It's the kind of unique Indigenous insistence on life from the imposition of death that springs from eternal attachment to land and clan.

Khadija Abu Lebdeh seemed to know from the beginning that she would write about her beloved brother. How she chose to remember and honor him in literature was stunning and moving. Muhammad Mu'ammar's story was a reminder to all of us that the things we dream about and wish for are not always what we need. He and Khadija were natural storytellers.

Abdallah Al-Sayyed wore a broad and persistent smile that belied his pain as a father and husband struggling to provide the minimal requirements of life for his family. Ali Abu Zayed was the same. Both of these men, though very different in disposition, writing styles, and the energy of their presence, reminded me of one another. They were kind, thoughtful, and generous, with a kind of abiding decency that sets the world right. They struggled to provide for their young families, but still showed up to all the workshops, committed to intellectual endeavors no matter the terrible circumstances. Samah Abu-Awwad is a poet at heart. The lyricism of her prose struck me, even more than her brilliant contribution itself.

In addition to allowing space for the senses, one of the things we focused on in our workshops was honesty—emotional, social, and political. I encouraged the writers to reach deep and not censor themselves when it came to that which may be taboo. Nebal Al-Najjar heeded that lesson, going against the grain of her kin and country in her desire to leave her home and never look back. It's natural to feel such things, and it doesn't mean one doesn't feel the exact opposite at other times or even simultaneously. I was proud of her for daring to write what the rest of the world, who expect us to be superheroes, may not want to hear from Palestinians. Likewise, Ali Abu Zayed started a second beautiful story about his quest to secure a small tent where he and his wife might find a moment of privacy and physical intimacy. I wish we could have added that story here, but life and responsibilities meant that Ali didn't have time to finish that story. Another story that moved me greatly was by a young man named Ghassan Salam. He was tall and broad and handsome, with the aura of gentleness. He only came to two of the workshops, but the first draft of his story stayed with me. The cries of the baby in his story that he could hear but not reach—somewhere in the open or under the rubble, where snipers crouched in waiting—still ring in my ear when I think of him. So does his agonizingly raw and honest internal dialogue when he said, "I am nothing." He was a natural writer. So I pursued and persisted. He had lost his phone where the first piece was stored, but he finally wrote another. And I am ever so glad he did. His piece is one of my favorites.

Huzama

As the original contributions were in Arabic, my instruction could only go so far. While I am literate in my mother tongue, I do not have a sophisticated command of Arabic to coach these writers linguistically. For that, my dear friend, the brilliant novelist Huzama Habayeb, stepped in.

I called her after I had already translated the entire collection—after Simon and Schuster offered us a contract, even. All prose needs editing, and I could not give them that, not in Arabic anyway. But she could, and she did.

Huzama put aside her own deadlines, her own work and family, and spent the next three months working with each writer. It was an experience unlike anything else for her, recorded in the editor's note of this anthology. She also recruited Kay Heikkinen, who likewise generously took time out of her busy schedule to help with the translation.

Real and raw

I am in awe and feel proud of each of the writers who attended the workshops and worked in impossible conditions without resources through both the writing and rewriting processes. They showed up in impossibly cruel circumstances to feel and experience moments of intellectual and creative exchange at a time when securing water and food demanded nearly the totality of their days. The evolution of their writing in a short time was remarkable, and I love every story here. They are raw and real, emotional and devastating. Each of them is a simple and common human moment, set during the holocaust of our time—buying bread, going to the toilet, mending a shoe, sharing a meal, finding transportation—all against the backdrop of the first live-streamed genocide, broadcast across the world in all its horror, gore, and ineffable suffering.

While these writers ostensibly came to learn from me, I was learning from them. I don't know what it's like to bury family without space to grieve; to see every building housing my memories become debris; to endure the humiliation and indignity of sharing a toilet with hundreds and fighting crowds for a cup of rice; to shiver in winter and collapse in summer inside a tent that offers no real protection; to be unable to provide or protect; to see death and hear its screams day in and day out.

But they do, and they showed me what it's like to gather up oneself to seek creativity and beauty.

I admire and respect them all. And it was my deep honor to impart whatever skills I have so these luminous sons and daughters of Palestine can be the ones to narrate this extraordinary moment in history, because it is their voices that matter the most. I don't know how to thank them or love them enough, except to put them in this book for the world to love them too.

A Note from the Editor, Huzama Habayeb

Between tahrir and tahrir: Another meaning for love

To write stories in the heart of an unfolding genocide is to draw ink from the depths of your own heart. To read stories of genocide, while the slaughter rages relentlessly, unceasingly, means that—at the very least—your heart will be crushed.

As the literary editor of this project, I don't think I was prepared to grapple with the magnitude of horror, devastation, and death lurking in every corner of Gaza—woven into a breathless narrative current that drags you under. It tightens your breath, and the space around you—wherever you are—shrinks, until you find yourself crammed into a tent, clutching a meager, violated, encroached life, surrounded by hollowed faces, whose features have melted away. In moments of raw storytelling, your pulse races under the savage Israeli bombardment that shakes the heavens and the earth, and you gather your flesh, terrified it will tear apart—only to realize that a soul, much like your own, has already been torn to shreds.

Since May 2025, for over three months, I have undertaken an extraordinary experience, perhaps the first literary editing process conducted entirely via WhatsApp, through daily discussions and follow-ups with eighteen writers in Gaza. I communicated with them remotely, between Amman and Dubai. I had to remain vigilant, alert to any message lighting up my phone screen in the dead of night or with the first rays of dawn, knowing how difficult it is for Gazans to communicate via mobile phones, as they have to wait for an internet signal to reach their devices or take a risk by traversing unsafe roads—in a land where no space is safe—just to charge their phones.

This was not merely a literary editing experience in the technical, linguistic, or structural sense; it was an emotional odyssey. The hardest moments came when I sent writers consecutive WhatsApp messages—guidance, suggestions for rephrasing, or inquiries about a specific meaning or character in their story—and then had to wait hours, sometimes days, for the message status to shift from a single gray tick to two, then to blue. In the space between gray and blue, my heart would pound, until the waiting itself became an obsession, my eyes glued to the phone screen, willing it to light up. Quite often, the most terrifying thought would creep into my mind: What if . . . ? But I refused to believe it.

It was a painful, shattering experience in its own way. What do you do when you ask someone to respond to a query as soon as possible, only to receive a delayed reply:

"I buried my wife yesterday; please bear with me until the mourning period ends."

Or:

"I'm ashamed to say . . . today we left everything behind and fled to the sea. We still haven't found a place to spend the night. Give me just three days, please, I beg your patience."

Or:

"If possible, I'll send the final version of the story on Saturday or Sunday . . . my brother was martyred."

How small, how utterly powerless I felt!

I—the mistress of words, as I like to call myself—found my own words failing me. My vocabulary of consolation collapsed into thin clichés—"My heart is with you," "Stay strong," or "Take care of yourself." Sometimes, it seemed as if I were giving a direct command: Stay alive!

And then I would feel ashamed of being alive.

Why should I live, while only a few hours away, a beautiful 22-year-old Palestinian woman—a promising writer and medical student with no college or university left to attend—has already in her young life endured 7 devastating Israeli invasions of Gaza, including the current genocide? She and her family have been displaced 13 times so far. She scrapes by with whatever work she can find to secure a sack of flour or lentils for her family of nine, their bodies gnawed by hunger. And when I ask how she is, she sends me a voice message that captures the sounds of shells and bullets from Israeli tanks and quadcopters as she walks to the hospital where she trains.

And yet, in a way, this experience was also liberating.

In Arabic, the word "tahrir" is wondrous. It carries two equally luminous meanings. On one hand, it means liberation, emancipation, release, the breaking of chains, both material and spiritual. On the other, it refers to the process of editing the drafts—especially literary editing, which involves addressing grammatical and structural issues, smoothing out the prose, and deepening its power. The two meanings, however, converge. For to edit a text is a form of liberating it from the constraints that bind its idea and message, so that it may soar into wider realms of expression.

If I owe anything to this emotional journey, to the difficult path I traversed with these remarkable creative writers, it is that their courage, passion, and determination to share their voices and stories amid the hell they endure, at any cost, liberated me.

When I wake to a message from one of them, a song she sang for me in a voice flowing with warmth and sweetness, or another reassuring me, saying, "Don't worry! I live by hope," I know that, today, I am free—freer than ever.

They will live.

They will dream.

They will love.

They will write.

This is their time—free Palestinians, born for life and for love.

Coffee by Old Blue

By Muhammad Mu'ammar

Details, too many details.

I don't know where to begin, or what to write about.

My heart used to pour words the moment I picked up a pen.

But today I am wordless, powerless to describe what I feel. What I endure.

This horror has drained us, exhausted us, ripped off our limbs and slit our throats from side to side.

I woke up, eyes half open, head buried in the pillow.

Another night of nightmares. Nothing new. Dread has been my constant companion, even in sleep, since the skies began raining bombs.

I've fought countless battles there, from attack to attack, before I wake up.

It took half an hour of wrestling with sunlight, my bedding, the faucet, and a sliver of soap before I woke up.

The word "faucet" is a metaphor now—a pail of meager water I scoop sparingly to splash on my face.

This ain't home. A minimal standard of living is nowhere to be found.

I am "displaced"—a benign word for utter human degradation!

I dwell in a triangular tent that I've fashioned from three posts and scraps of cloth.

Frankly, it's not a tent in the proper sense, but something close enough.

It's true I can't stand upright inside it. And my feet push against it if I lie down fully.

But at least it shelters me and my family from the cold and the fire.

—interpret "*fire*" however you wish.

And speaking of fire . . . naturally, I light it as soon as I wake up.

It has become an eternal morning ritual, without which the day holds no blessing.

The era of fuel and gas is gone. Primitive life reigns here!

Its reign is so absolute that I no longer wonder, *What will the future be like?*

Instead, *What comes after this?*

When will the Stone Age begin?

And, *Will we go further back still?*

Morning thoughts before the fire are strange. Don't you agree?

Well then. Fine. Enough of my rambling—come drink with me the coffee I brew whenever I light the flames.

Coffee we now buy by the gram, after a lifetime of buying it in kilograms.

I tried to give it up. I really did. But I couldn't.

Coffee is a part of my soul, my pen, my very being.

I made it today especially to help me write.

As always, I carried it with me to visit Old Blue, my friend and companion since I was a child.

Ah, Gaza's Sea!

I had always dreamed of living near the sea. And now I do.

My dream came true at last, but not as I dreamed.

I came to Old Blue displaced, running for our lives, everything lost behind.

I came to him weeping, carrying in my chest the tears of the world.

I came reproaching him—

Why do you welcome me in times like these?

Why call me beside you under drones and missiles, and not birds and sunshine?

But before I could berate it further, I understood—

he's like me—or maybe I'm like him.

We both suffer, each in his own way.

I sat silent in his presence, contemplating him, thinking of the home I abandoned.

Thinking of my separation from family, loved ones, and friends.

Thinking of my uncles, my aunts, my cousins—their faces flickered before my eyes, those who were suddenly gone.

They did not leave gently.

They were wrenched away. Brutally. Cruelly. By a single missile from a spiteful plane flown by a pilot as hateful as the missile and plane.

Thirty souls or more.

We pulled them from the rubble in pieces, shards, and fragments.

Torn flesh of men mixed with that of women and children.

Three days we spent gathering their body parts from the ground, from beneath it, from the rooftops of neighboring homes.

Then came the miracle—one that brought joy to everyone and simultaneously doubled the pain.

A single child survived. My cousin.

They told him his family was fine.

He said he saw his father blown to bits.

He felt relief when he found his mother in intensive care.

They exchanged tender words.

But tenderness vanished, and the brief light in his eyes dimmed when his mother followed his father into death.

He prayed his little sister was still alive.

They told him she was martyred with their father that same night.

What heart can bear such pain?

I wept bitterly at his patience—for the endurance of this child through these blows, one after another.

I died a thousand deaths with his father, my uncle, and his mother and sister, as I watched innocence fade from his small face.

A boy not yet twelve, his heart so aged he was almost forty.

I wiped my tears that rained at this memory, only to be struck by another: a family fleeing their home in fear of shelling wiped out completely, while the house remained standing as it was, untouched, unscathed by anything.

I sleep and wake to the heaviest memories pressing on my heart.

Often, I wish I could sleep and never wake up.

My memories with Old Blue were once wonderful, full of the living faces I loved.

Now I sit with him alone, my cup of coffee brimming with loss, and still more loss, and loss that cuts deep.

Yes, I know wars and injustice have happened, happen now, and will go on happening across the world. That savage death is a hideous human reality.

I know well, as we were taught when we were little, that the whole world will one day vanish.

Yes, I believe in that, despite everything.

But do you know where my private tragedy lies amid all the horrors happening in this patch of earth?

My greatest wound—the one that rips open my chest?

After I said farewell to my wife and buried her with these two hands. . . .

I do not dare call her name now.

I'm afraid that if I call her name and she doesn't answer, I will have to believe that she is truly gone.

Gone and left me.

Like so many have gone before her.

Old Blue was witness to our most tender moments together. My wife and me and Old Blue.

In his silence, he knows the cruel anguish I suffer.

I don't yet know if I can bear it.

I'm alone now, my old friend.

I've returned to you as I once was—with no one in my life but you, my words, and my coffee.

But this time I've come back to become like you.

An old blue soul.

An immensity of silence.

Everyday

By Reema Abu Mousa

Returning from a futile, exhausting errand, I couldn't find transportation to Al-Awda intersection in Rafah. I had no choice but to walk the last 2 kilometers.

My mother called: "Where are you, my love? Thank God there's a signal; I've been calling you for two hours. I was afraid something happened, God forbid!"

"I swear, transportation is a nightmare, Mama. Only God knows."

"Alright, sweetheart. It's getting dark. Hurry home."

I watched the faces of people passing, one after the other—each etched with the same bleak misery. They walked in a daze, as if they'd been taken from the world they knew—a normal, familiar, deeply human world—and hurled into a waking nightmare. I should have been getting ready for my graduation from the College of Pharmacy. Now I didn't look forward to the next hour, let alone tomorrow.

My mother was still on the line. "Alloo? Are you there?"

"I'm here, Mama. I'm on the way." I told her not to worry and promised to be careful before we hung up.

A clamor rose from the dusty street, led by a donkey-cart driver, shouting "Watch your back! Move, watch your back!" Like everyone, I stepped aside to avoid getting hit.

After walking nearly half an hour, a battered van stopped—a vehicle that used to haul goods before the genocide, but had been transformed into transport for people since.

The driver asked where I was headed. "Al Awda intersection," I told him.

He waved his hand. "Get in!"

One of the passengers slid open the side door. I was stunned by the scene. People were piled up in every available spot.

"Where am I supposed to get in?" I asked.

It occurred to me to walk away, but I quickly dismissed the idea. I might not find another ride. I tried not to look flustered or add to the discomfort of the other passengers as they shifted around to make room for me. The only spot they managed was a cramped sliver between a girl around 10 years in an old wheelchair—her leg amputated and her face dazed, like she was watching stuck in a nightmare—and a man in his fifties, dissolving in shame as he shrank back to keep his flesh from touching mine.

The van took off, its weary tires dragging over a road laden with dread and ominous possibilities. I scanned the faces around me. They all shared the same expression of sorrow.

Across from me, a mother struggled to quiet her child, who was insisting on something, I didn't know what, which she apparently could not give him. Beside her, an old woman muttered curses against whoever had brought us to this state. In the back, a group of young men vented about soaring prices and the profiteering we were all enduring.

The van stopped suddenly.

"Alright, everyone. Ker intersection. Everybody off. I'm turning back here," the driver shouted.

As the passengers began filing off quietly, I protested.

"I'm not getting off here, Uncle. I need to get to Al Awda intersection."

"Al Awda is packed," he snapped back testily, as if I should already know the situation. "Walk the rest of the way; it's just a couple of steps."

I had no choice. And anyway, no one else was complaining.

"Fine, trust in God!" I said and disembarked.

I walked the rest of the way, grumbling to myself, "God damn transportation, damn the roads, damn the people, damn this horror, damn life and its father! Good God, damn it all!"

I was ranting out loud like a lunatic. "A couple of steps?! A couple of steps, man? All this way is a couple of steps? Since when did 2 kilometers turn into a couple of steps? Pretty soon we'll be crossing the whole country on foot, because why not? It's all just a couple of steps, right?!"

I got home half an hour later. "Yamma!" I called out to my mother as soon as I entered. "Where are you? What do we have to eat? What did you cook?"

"Is that any way to talk?" My mother's reply was something between reprimand and resignation. "Beans and rice."

I wasn't fond of that dish, but it had become a staple in our bleak new reality. Little did we know that this dish would soon become a luxury, a nostalgic memory at a time when we would consume anything remotely edible.

I watched my mother as she portioned the food in plates, one for each of us.

"There are two pieces of pita left," she said to me. "Eat one and leave the other for your sister Alaa."

Alaa was on the autism spectrum. She couldn't eat just anything we had; she was intensely picky and only accepted certain foods. The last time our flour ran out, she cried hysterically, as if we were deliberately denying her food. Terms like "running out of flour," "ration coupons," "individual allotment," "waiting," "patience," "shortage," "finding a substitute," "emergency," even "war"—all beyond her comprehension.

My mother did her utmost to give her food suited to her dietary needs. We didn't want to think about what would happen the day there might be no food for her at all.

Exhausted and dragging my feet, I said to my mother, "Tell

one of my sisters to get my plate ready while I pray, so I can sleep after. And no one wake me up!"

"What do you think this is, a hotel?" my mother shot back angrily. "Get out of my sight!"

Thus, a small scene I relive every day—one called "transportation." Our lives have become a constant sprint for the bare necessities.

One later morning, I rode in a donkey cart with a group of women and young men to a distant distribution center, hoping to get a food coupon.* I returned at the end of that long day empty-handed, boiling with rage, my blood seething with frustration, as if fire was about to erupt from within me and burn the whole world down.

Where did the word "coupon" even come from? I wondered. A new word had snuck into our lives and Gaza's vocabulary. We all know it—it's on the lips of young and old alike. I hear it dozens of times a day. It invaded us. Occupied us. It's our first thought when we open our eyes in the morning and the last thing on our minds before we sleep.

I laid my head on the pillow, already planning tomorrow's journey. I'd arranged with a college friend to go together to collect food coupons from a distribution center about an hour's walk away.

Like every day, the Palestinian march toward the coupon lines begins at dawn in Gaza—bodies depleted, spirits crushed, eyes wide and empty. Zombies on their way to their resurrection.

---

*"coupon" is the word aid organizations use to refer to rations.

His Name Is Salam

By Khuloud Abu Zaher

Three o'clock in the morning. She sits at a stiff angle, propped against a pillow as dark and bruised as the future. The crystalline silence keeps her company. Her face is swollen and pale, ringed with shadows. Sweat beads down her skin. Her cracked feet rest atop a mat as tattered as everything around her.

On the left, her husband lies awake, stirred by the soft mist of love and a tender intuition deep within him. Wide-eyed and unblinking, he scans her quickly.

"Looks like it's time. What can I do?" he says.

"I want my mother," she responds in a hoarse, sharp voice.

She softens gradually, her eyes filling with tears, and silence settles again.

Conflicted, he murmurs with sorrow, "You know your mother is still trapped in Gaza City. Coming here to the south isn't easy."

He kisses her softly on the cheek, not enough to ease her labor pains or make up for the absence of her mother, but because it's the only comfort he can offer.

His kiss stirs her to rise. Standing in the center of the tent, she tries to gather fragments of advice still clinging to the walls of memory, hoping they'll be enough to guide her through her first childbirth.

Though deliverance draws near, she moans in silence. The pain intensifies—sometimes she clasps her back; other times she leans helplessly against the tent's flimsy frame. She screams into a void, unheard, and curses the myth of motherhood in a rebel land, where nothing is allowed to grow, then grow more, and grow still—before it dies.

Thirty minutes pass between contractions—enough time to inspect her armpits and other parts of her body. "Ugh! the hair's grown back. I need to remove it," she mutters to herself.

She moves heavily, rummaging among the bags piled in the corner of the tent for a razor—a substitute for the costly boiled sugar wax—and for scented wipes in place of scarce water.

Then she checks the baby's bag: summer clothes in December—absurd and telling. Most are used, the rest donations. Two handmade cloth sanitary pads cut from dark fabric. Two diapers. It all makes her feel ashamed of how little welcome awaits her newborn.

The temperamental winter sun comes through their miserable tent, drying the dew that clung to its nylon plastic roof. She feels the morning light has thrown her a lifeline, saving her from a nighttime delivery that could cost her her life, or the baby's, or both.

Now the pain is ferocious. It's time to choose her transportation to the hospital as the labor escalates—a donkey or horse-drawn cart? Or a three-wheeled tuktuk? None is cheap, and all come with terms set by the driver.

They settle on a horse-drawn cart, the most fitting for her condition. No sooner does she escape from the crowd of pedestrians, after an endless wait, than she is trapped again—this time in crowds of those carrying the martyred, injured, and sick through the hospital hallways.

But it's no ordinary crowding. Everything is strewn and scattered here—people, human dignity, safety, serenity, love, everything . . . everything.

She freezes. The pain of labor subsides in solidarity before the horror of the scene. A funeral prayer is underway over rows of body bags and shrouds containing corpses and collected body parts. Among them is an infant, wrapped in white. She instinctively puts a hand on her belly and moves away, anxious and disturbed.

Blood stains everything. It seems perverse and indecent that the color of roses and love should be red. The corridors overflow with bodies and open wounds. Doctors, staff, all are endlessly running. Ambulance sirens wail without pause, keeping pace with every explosion.

A voice yells at her: "You have to go to the maternity ward. It's now in the back building. The front one is for the dead and wounded."

She mutters again, "God, when will this day end?"

Leaning on her husband's shoulder, she climbs the stairs—step by heavy step—until she finally reaches the delivery room.

She sees a fetal heart monitor, tools for natural childbirth, and iron-framed beds separated by white curtains that obscure sight but not sound, nor the circumstances surrounding each birth—a child named after his martyred father; a mother crying, "I don't want to give birth while we're living in a tent"; another, sobbing with joy or grief—she can't tell; a grandmother ululating, delighted by her first grandson after five granddaughters.

She climbs onto the bed. Her child begins a final battle for life, perhaps believing this life is something precious, worth clinging to.

The pain intensifies, more and more, one jolt after another. Her body convulses with each contraction. Her face tightens with every surge.

"Come on . . . breathe in, breathe out . . . breathe in, breathe out," the doctor helps and instructs her. "There's only a little bit left, push . . . push!"

Then, a cry—the sound of a new life. A new voice. A voice that insists on life despite everything. A round face. Fair skin tinted in red, as if touched with henna. Black hair. Wide brown eyes. Rosy lips. Flushed cheeks.

A prophet proclaiming our survival, assuring us we will remain. The doctor smiles and teases, "What will you name this little troublemaker?"

She exhales in a sigh. "Salam," she says. "I will name him Salam."

Ma'rouf

By Ghassan Salam

Like all bitterly cold nights, this one was stripped bare, draped only in a dense darkness without end. Time meandered without passing, and death hovered over us in every direction.

War is cruel. It devours our souls, steals our dreams, skins us alive, and pushes us out of our own lives, our own essence—leaving us lost within our bodies, strangers even to ourselves, to the version of us we once knew.

You feel locked in a race against your own demise, scrambling for escape—conjuring steps out of illusion, just to keep the earth from shutting its doors on you. But soon you are conquered by your own helplessness. What strength could possibly hold its ground against such torment? What human can outpace this death?

I still live every moment as if it were that night—the night we fled our home in Khan Younis and entered the clamor of terror and panic. I left without saying goodbye to anything, and everything I once knew cast me out, as if I were a child of the open, abandoned to the bare world.

I felt blind before the horrors I saw, as if my eyes refused to believe, choosing instead to trade their light for darkness rather than let my heart be slaughtered.

But there was no escape. All my senses awakened.

There's no time for rest, no retreat from the scene. Every part of you must bear witness. How could all of this be real? Why us?

This calamity is unbearably heavy—heavier than us, heavier than the sum of all our sorrows.

I hid from Zionist fire inside a greenhouse covered in transparent plastic. Before us lay an open field, its features blurred by the night. Despite the roar of explosions, the earth-shaking air strikes around us, the relentless buzz of drones, I heard the cry of a baby in the direction of the open field.

My heart leapt from its place, and my hands flew toward the sound, ready to soothe, to rescue. But the sky was furious, pouring a wrath upon us, as if determined to sever any human connection that might still be salvaged.

Warplanes lit up everything around us—not with light, but with fire. The blaze illuminated a scene: a family of four—a man, a woman, and two children. One child lay beside the father, the other nestled in his mother's arms. She had likely been running, clutching her baby to her chest, when a shell tore through her back and brought her down. Her arms, even in death, remained wrapped protectively around her child. The baby cried out, pleading for his mother. But she was silent. And the crying pierced my heart.

I tried to move, but death's reach was closer than the family. I feared for the child—if I went toward him, we might both be killed. But maybe, just maybe, I could save him. I didn't want to lose the chance.

The shelling intensified, the baby's cries rising and fading. I felt a flicker of hope each time his cry grew loud, and when the cries quieted, I lashed myself with blame and guilt until my breath tore to shreds, ragged and gasping.

An hour passed. Then two. Then three.

My eyelids grew heavy, and the baby's whimpering grew tired. Silence settled, until I was awakened by the sun. The night shed its terror at last, though its darkness still lingered in the depths of my soul.

I was exhausted and trembling, but my heart propelled me to reach the family. Not one of them stirred—not even the baby. I leaned in—perhaps the sun might awaken them too. But they had drowned in yesterday's darkness. Drowned in blood. In death.

It was only moments before the Israeli warplanes returned, conquering the sky once more. I felt as if a massive ball of yarn began to wind thick wool threads around my head, blinding me, choking my breath, pushing through my mouth, locking my voice. My blood froze, my body paralyzed. I stood there, limp and helpless.

Just as defeat and surrender began to overtake me, the baby's cry rang out again. A jolt of life surged through me, melting its paralysis and unraveling the woolen yarn. Blood rushed back into my limbs, my breath came alive, and I broke free from fear. My mind lodged in my legs, fast and daring. For the first time, my body acted without hesitation. It charged forward—steady, focused, and sharp, like a falcon.

I pulled the baby—a toddler perhaps a year old or more—from his mother's arms and fled as fast as I could. I didn't look at him. My eyes were fixed on the sky, scanning for drones or fighter jets that might strike us both, but never losing sight of the path ahead. I don't know how long I ran before I reached a house that might shelter us, my little one and me—though its roof, like all roofs and skies in Gaza, offered no safety. The house was abandoned, clearly not so long ago. I moved through it like a thief intruding on the sanctity of someone else's home.

Only then did I inspect the baby. He stole my heart the moment my eyes fell on him. He was asleep, like an angel—no, like children are meant to sleep. Peacefully. He looked like a blossom of soft cotton, nestled in a field of serenity, unaware that his roots had just been ripped from the soil.

And now, what do I do?

I turned in circles, searching. I thought of laying him on a mattress, but I hesitated—rather, I feared for him. He was now in my care.

I began to move with a mother's heart. In the kitchen, I found some scraps of leftover food on the table to ease my own hunger. But from now on, there was a stomach the size of an egg that needed to be filled first.

I scoured the house for anything the baby could eat, then returned to the kitchen, searching the cupboards and refrigerator for milk. I found some herbs and boiled anise. I think its scent must have tickled the little creature's nose and woke him. I tried to cool the drink quickly, but how could I feed it to him? I rummaged through drawers and found a bag of syringes. It was the only solution.

I watched his face as he drank from the syringe. His tiny fingers curled around mine. What was this feeling? Something I had never experienced before seeped into me, warm and tender. It made me forget time, forget the fear.

There was nothing more I could give my little one. I had to leave the house—for every standing building in Gaza was a target.

I stepped out, holding the baby close to my heart. In my other hand, a bag of food I'd taken from the house, apologizing silently to its owners.

I walked quickly, my little one dozing in my arms. Eventually, I made it somewhere where there were others like me—shocked, worn, bearing the same haunted look.

I headed to a school that'd become a refugee shelter. There were no classrooms left that could take in more displaced people, so I claimed a patch of ground in the schoolyard for me and my little one.

They registered me as a displaced person. The baby, whose name or family I didn't know, was registered as an orphan of unknown lineage, based on my testimony about the death of his family.

They asked me to choose a provisional name for him for official registration.

A strange fit of laughter overcame me—the hysterical sort born of grief, laughter that tries to hide sobs.

I contemplated the weight of this responsibility I had taken on just a day earlier.

"Ma'rouf," I said. "I'll name him Ma'rouf."*

It took two days to find my family, as we had been separated in the chaos of fleeing. The enemy had scattered us, each of us chasing survival.

They were in another school-shelter. Fortunately, they had gotten half a classroom to themselves. They were anxiously awaiting my arrival, welcoming me into their warmth. And Ma'rouf too, when they heard our story.

My sister cared for my little one while we inquired and tried to find information about his family. But the invasion of Khan Younis dragged on. No one could return.

I counted the days, longing to go back home with my family. Life was hard and harsh, but Ma'rouf filled it with his light and ethereal presence.

The invasion ended in April 2024. How joyful the news—and how heavy it was on my heart. Unlike others, I did not return to my home. I went back to the scene of the crime.

Finally, at the spot where I had rescued Ma'rouf, I began to sweat. My hands went numb, and it was hard for me to breathe. Panic and fear seized me again, and I sank deep into them. Lying there were human remains—fragments of bodies and bones.

---

*Ma'rouf can have two meanings. It can mean "known"—a counter to the child being registered as "unknown." Ma'rouf can also mean "a kindness," "a favor," or "a good deed."

I thanked God that no one had reached the site before me. I searched scattered clothing and found personal documents—identification papers belonging to Ma'rouf's family.

At last, Ma'rouf would be known. I read the names, folded the papers, and slipped them into my pocket. I returned to the school-shelter, rejoining Ma'rouf and my family.

Ma'rouf's real name was Adam. The first son. The origin of it all. How could anyone call him unknown?

For a week, I avoided speaking about Ma'rouf, until my father sat me down, insisting we find surviving relatives and return the child to his kin.

Why, Baba? Why do you tie my heart to the gallows?

But it had to be done. I mustered the strength to inquire about his extended family—a grandfather, an uncle, someone?

Ten days later, I found his uncle. He didn't believe me. The man nearly lost his mind. At last, a trace of his brother's bloodline had been found.

And me? What would I be without Ma'rouf? He had claimed an immense part of my life, of my days.

His family came for him. He was too young to understand. And I was too young to bear such pain.

• • •

Three months after my little one was taken from me, I was scrolling through my phone when I saw the news: the house where Adam lived with his uncle had been bombed!

Again, panic and fear.

I rushed to the scene.

What had I done? Had I saved him only to send him back into death's jaws?

If only I hadn't!

I reached the bombing site. It felt like the end—like a hand was crushing my neck.

Ahhh! Why, O God? Why?

Civil defense medics were pulling out the dead and wounded.

I recognized him by his little toes. I had kissed them so many times. I knew those tiny feet by heart. I found myself with him in the ambulance. Ma'rouf was alive. Injured, but alive. I thanked God and I wept.

I never left his side at the hospital. No one was left from his uncle's family—all of them killed. But my little one, the son of my heart, survived.

Life returned to me once more. Morning returned. Time returned. Ma'rouf returned to me—if only for a while.

• • •

Six months later, an unknown number appeared on my phone. Something sank in my chest.

—Hello?

—Yes.

—Is this Brother Sami?

—Yes, who's speaking?

—Na'eema, young Adam's paternal aunt.

What?

Where had she come from?

He's not Adam anymore.

He's Ma'rouf.

This time no one will take him from me.

I spoke, unable to hide the edge in my voice:

—I didn't know he had a living aunt.

—I'm in northern Gaza—Jabalia. I learned about a month ago that my nephew survived and was in your care.

—Fine. What do you want now?

—I want to take him.

I clenched my anger.

—There are no open roads open between the north and the south.

I was trying to push the thought out of her head, but she answered with calm insistence.

—I'll wait until I can reach Adam.

A truce was declared less than two weeks later, and the roads reopened. It was as if the whole world was conspiring to take away my son.

The aunt came.

And she took Ma'rouf.

This time, my family and I were not okay. Ma'rouf had brought a new sense of joy and love into our lives. Our souls had grown attached to him. He had become our child.

Less than two months later, Israel's aggression started again—more savage and brutal than ever. And the burdens grew heavier.

The distance between us and Ma'rouf became vast and untraversable. I stayed in touch with him through video calls, but I felt shy to express how much I loved and missed him in front of his family. I also worried he might sense my fear and weakness—he who had only known smiles and laughter from me.

He could speak more words now. In every call, he begged me to come see him, and I would promise I would. But I knew I couldn't keep that promise. How do you explain to your child that what separates isn't distance—but death after death after death?

The events of genocide piled up. The days blurred together. And life thinned out. My thoughts always ran to my son. I became like a little boy, one that grown-ups could soothe with tricks. But I was the grown-up too, tricking myself with sweet words and false hope to silence my grief.

• • •

It was one in the afternoon. I was with a few friends at a nearby café, one of the rare places with electricity and internet. We exchanged news and endless stories—so horrific they barely seemed real.

We sat sipping coffee, watching the screen, when breaking news appeared: An Israeli air strike had just hit Jabalia, in northern Gaza. A man on a bicycle had been targeted. Many dead. Many wounded. I saw bodies scattered in the street, through the screen.

I scanned every face, my heart pounding with every image, racing ahead of the scenes flashing on the television.

Then I saw him.

Yes, I knew it was him. How could I not recognize the boy my eyes had memorized? Whose imprint was engraved in my heart and whose soul was braided into mine?

Ma'rouf was gone. And I was left behind.

In truth, I too had gone. And never returned.

A Trail of Soap

By Diana Islayh

I poured yellow liquid dish soap into my left palm, which instinctively cupped into a deep hollow, like a well yearning to be a well once more. I would need to wash my hands after using the toilet near our tent, though the faucet was usually empty. Water had been annihilated alongside people in this genocide, becoming a ghost that graciously deigns to appear to us when it wishes to—one we chase after rather than flee.

The miserable toilet was made of four wooden posts, wrapped in a makeshift curtain made from an old scrap of fabric—so sheer you could see silhouettes behind it, like some obscene farce mimicking the absurdity of our lives. A blanket full of holes and splinters served as a "door."

Inside, a concrete slab with a hole in the middle. You need time to convince yourself to enter such a place. The stench alone seizes your eyelids and turns your stomach the moment it creeps into your nose.

I thought about going to the damned, distant public toilet. I hated it during the first weeks of our displacement, but it was the only one in the area where you could both relieve yourself and scrub off the dust of misery that clung to every air molecule.

It infuriated me that it was wretched and run-down, and the crowding only made it worse—full of sand, soiled toilet paper and sanitary pads scattered in every corner.

My imagination recoiled from the routing of going to this women's public toilet, about 50 meters from our tent.

"Should I go?" I asked myself, aloud.

I decided to go, taking one step forward and two steps back. I'd ask anyone returning from the toilet, "Is there water in the tap today?" and await the answer with the eagerness of a child hoping for candy.

"You have to hurry before it runs out!"

Or, more often, "There isn't any."

So we'd all—men, women, and children—arm ourselves with a plastic water bottle, which was a kind of public declaration: "*We're off to the toilet.*" We'd also carry a bar of soap in a box, although most people didn't bother using it since it didn't lather and was like washing your hands with a rock.

I looked up and exhaled, staring into the vast gray nothingness that stared right back at me. Then I stepped out onto the sand across from our ramshackle displacement camp—Karama, "Camp Dignity"—though dignity itself cries out in this filthy, exhausted place, choked with chaos and a desperate scramble to moisten our veins with a drop of life.

The road was empty, as it was early morning, and even the clamor of camp life lay dormant at that hour. Still, I couldn't relax my shoulders—to signal my senses that we were alone, that we were safe. My fingers remained clenched over the yellow dish soap, my hand hanging at my side to keep it from spilling.

I crossed the distance to the toilet—step by step, meter by meter, tent by tent and the souls who dwelled in them, just as they were, unchanged, their curious eyes fixed on me. I passed a garbage heap, shaped like a crescent moon, overflowing with all kinds of empty food cans—food that had ruined the linings of our intestines and united us in the agonies of digestion and bowel movements.

Something trickled from my palm—a thread of liquid that felt like blood dripping between my fingers, down my wrist in thickening droplets. My hand trembled, and my eyes blurred. I convinced myself—without looking—that it was all in my head, not in my hand, quickened my pace, my heartbeat thudding in my ears.

At last, I reached the only two public toilets in the area, one for men and the other for women, both encased in white plastic printed with the blue UNICEF logo.

Inside, I was met with the "toilet chronicles"—no less squalid than the toilet itself—unparalleled chatter among women who'd waited long hours in the line together.

The old women bemoaned the soft nature of our generation, insisting our condition was a "moral consequence" of our being spoiled.

Other women pleaded to be let into the toilet quickly because they were diabetic. They banged on the door with urgency and physical pain, like they would break in and grab the person behind it by the throat, shouting, "When will you come out?!"

The woman inside yelled back, "I'm squeezing my guts out! Should I vomit them up too? Have patience! Damn whoever called this a 'rest room'!"

I looked around. A pale-faced woman smiled at me. I returned her smile, but my face quickly stiffened again, as if the muscles scolded me for stretching them into a smile. A voice inside me whispered meanly, *What are you both even smiling about?*

A furious cry rang from the other stall, "Oh my God! Someone is plucking her body hair! What are you doing, you bitch? It's a toilet! A toilet!"

Another voice shot back, "Lower your voice, woman, and hurry up! The child's crying!"

Two little girls stood nearby, with tousled hair, drool marking their cheeks, their eyes half shut. They were crying to use the toilet, clutching their crotches, shifting restlessly in the sandy corridor where we stood.

I was trying to push through to the water tap at the end of the hall, attempting to escape this tiresome, tragic theater. As my luck would have it, there was no water. I opened my palm. It too was empty. The yellow dish soap my mother bought yesterday was gone. All that remained was a sticky smear across my left hand and a long thread trailing behind me in the sand. *Had it been dripping from my hand all along the way?*

I twisted the faucet handle back and forth—a futile hope for even a thin thread of water. Not a single drop came.

My body sagged under the weight of rage, disappointment, fury, and a storm of unanswerable questions. I rushed through the crowded corridor of angry women, out into the street. I couldn't hold back tears.

I wept.

I wept with all my being and soul.

I cursed the whole world, humanity, civilization, people.

I cursed myself and the occupation and Gaza and her sea—the sea I love with a weary, lonely love, just as I've always loved everything in this patch of earth.

I sobbed the entire way back. Without shame. I didn't care who saw—not the passersby, not the homes or tents, not the ground I walked on. My grief rained tears on this land on my way there and back.

But the land's thirst is never quenched—neither with our tears, nor with our blood.

My eyes were wrung dry from crying by the time I reached our tent. I collapsed on the ground, like a warrior who drops to his knees on the battlefield, gutted by swords, his blood and hope spilled.

Questions clamored in my head.

Can a homeland also be exile?

Can another exile exist within exile?

What is home?

Is home the homeland itself, the soil of a nation?

Or is it the other way around—the homeland is only so if it's truly home?

If the homeland is the home, why do I feel like a stranger in Rafah—a place just ten minutes from my city, Khan Younis?

And why did I fear the feeling I had when I imagined myself in our kitchen, where my mother cooked mulukhiya and maqluba for the first time in six months, even though I wasn't at home—in our house?

That day, I said aloud, "Is this what the occupation wants? For me to feel 'at home' merely in the memory of home?"

How can I feel at home without being there?

How can I be outside of my homeland when I'm in it?

I looked down at my hand—dry and cracked with January's chill. The yellow soap liquid had turned into frozen white powder between my fingers.

My Room

By Saja Laham

The city was sorrowful. Everything within it mourned. The sky trembled with the terror of Israeli drones. The sun hid behind thick clouds. Even the air was taut with anxiety. Relentless warplane bombardment made my heart pound hard and fast. Israeli tanks were only a few meters from our home.

What next? What will happen to us? Where will we go? Questions crawled and collided in my head.

Fear gripped the city. "Nuzuh"—displacement—was on every father's lips, each one haunted by dread for his family. My father was no different.

My mother and I packed a bag for each of my brothers—their official papers and warm clothes for this bitter cold. I turned to my own bag, my heart heavy with rage. Standing before my wardrobe, full of beautiful, expensive clothes, I studied them in silence.

What do I take? What do I leave behind?

I am the oldest child in the family, the only girl among five brothers, spoiled by them all. My father never spared us any luxury—clothes, gifts, anything we wanted.

How do I abandon my home? All the things dear to my heart?

I scanned my desk, nestled under the window overlooking the neighborhood. It held my notebooks, university textbooks, colored pens of every kind. It was lined with sticky notes bearing motivational phrases I'd repeat to myself, sometimes even hum them like a song.

Here I believed in my dream and began.

Rise, rise, and face the hard days. Some days will smile upon you, others will push against you. That's life, one day heavy, one day triumphant. Rise and make your way.

I had arranged my desk with care. My gaze lingered on my books—books I'd have to leave behind. I wondered if they would survive the obliteration crushing our flesh and our spirit. My dream had been to graduate from university and become a teacher. It was my family's dream too. But all that collapsed, buried alongside the world I knew, in the rubble of what was once our home. The occupation army forced us all from our homes. *Damned Zionists. May they be cursed!* I wept bitterly, muttering fury through tears.

With the gentleness of a mother caressing a child's face, I wiped away the dust that had settled on my books from the shelling nearby and hid them in my closet.

When my bag was ready, I gave my room one last lingering look, bidding farewell to all the memories it held. The tape of my life, already so short, flashed before my eyes, and I wept once again.

It broke my heart to leave. My room was my refuge, my own home within our home. I closed the door as I always did, clinging to the hope that one day I'd return. That hopeful days would return. That life would return, and my dreams will wait for me.

Every Moment Is a Life

By Rizq Ahmad

In this era stripped of tenderness, where aggression knows no end and the bleeding of death never stops, affection and warmth among displaced families have become a sort of luxury. As we all sink into the mire of the daily struggle just to survive, we keep moving from one place to another, clinging to a life that bears no resemblance to anything truly alive.

The colors of places began to fade, dissolving into the same gray rubble. The joy of our recent past slipped through our fingers, and memories of yesterday fell through the tattered holes in our souls.

We left behind a large house—with an even larger heart. It held our stories, our dreams, our celebrations, and our sorrows. I remember it as if from another life: lying on my bed, the air sagging with the scent of coconut oil, planning my day in a diary, jotting down the details of my life—the ordinary and fleeting ones, and those that carried meaning, if only to me.

Then, as if life had suddenly turned a page to a nightmare, a call from the Israeli military—just a few seconds long—forced us to abandon our beautiful home, its elegant rooms bearing my mother's gentle touches.

We found ourselves in a makeshift nylon shack—one side transparent, barely shielding us, and the other black, trapping us in suffocating heat. We pieced it together from old fabric scraps:

my late grandmother's dresses and children's blankets adorned with superheroes who once lit up our childhood rooms.

But it didn't end there. That shack, shared by four families, became a traveling shelter that we carried from one so-called "safe zone" to another. At first, we dubbed it "The Four Winds." Later, we changed it to "The Four Coupons," a nod to the four food-aid vouchers from relief organizations. The voucher colors changed with each renewal, but we remained the same—stuck in misery, in need, and in a futile, endless wait.

The decision to flee from one area to another was always made collectively. Each time, the discussion centered on two questions: When do we leave? And where do we go? Meanwhile, we did all we could—armed with caution and a bit of luck—to avoid Israeli air strikes and dodge their shelling. In truth, we could never tell where the strikes would land, or when, or how.

A small rickety wooden table in our shack would turn into a war room—an emergency operations conference. We would gather around it—grandfather, parents, siblings, children, and grandchildren—beating with one heart, making life-altering decisions.

Most mornings began early—earlier than they used to—with the calls of vendors cutting through a sky thick with the buzz of zanana drones, selling milk and bread around the camp. We shared our meager food, and everyone shouldered the daily responsibilities of cooking and cleaning. At night, we laughed as we arranged our bedding on the ground, filing our bodies close in the cramped space to snatch a few hours of sleep.

There was no mirror in the shack. If any of us wanted to check our appearance, we turned to my mother, Hanan, the gentle queen of our hearts, the mirror who always saw us as beautiful and handsome, no matter how we looked. I struck a pose before my older sister, Hala, who bursts out laughing at the sight of my pants, barely clinging to my waist, the belt wrapped around it one and a half times. As I was about to step outside, my brother Adam called after me:

"Don't stay out long! I need the pants later."

When I returned to the shack, I saw the tired faces of the grandkids—my nieces and nephews. Their skin scorched by the summer sun, they wore mismatched clothes that didn't distinguish boy from girl. Their eyes brimmed with hunger, weariness, and a quiet patience for whatever aid might have trickled into our camp.

"What's for lunch today?" I asked my sister Hanadi.

She flashed a small smile while stirring the pot. "Fasoolia beans. But we can only make enough rice for the children. The grown-ups can eat the fasoolia with bread," she replied.

Hanadi had taken over the cooking to spare our mother from the heat of fire in this burning weather. "I'll make a salad too, but without tahini. It's expensive," she added.

Hanadi cooked with love, and her salad was unmatched.

Our world today measures no more than a single square meter—barely enough space for us to sit together. The aroma of onions and broth from bouillon cubes—our substitute for meat—filled the air. One of us gingerly wiped the table, mindful of the nails jutting out like thorns.

Baba called us to eat. Even in displacement, gathering as a family for a meal—whether around a ramshackle table or a threadbare mat on the ground—was sacred.

Baba had prepared a beloved dish of finely chopped onions and spices, garnished with a scatter of minced basil leaves, fiery green chilies, and garlic in a mouthwatering, vibrant tableau.

"There's talk of a truce," my eldest brother, Hisham, announced the good news with exaggerated optimism.

Seasoning the food, the rickety chair groaning beneath him and the stove's heat hemming him, Baba said, "God is great. As long as you are all safe, everything else can be endured."

We fetched whatever fruit we could find and placed it on the table.

Baba reminded us: "Eat sparingly, so there's enough bread for everyone and no one says they're hungry."

Of course, the dishes had to be washed and polished—a rule we carried from our pre-displacement life. The lunch table transformed into a roundtable for political debate. We argued and analyzed the course of the aggression as if on a live talk show like "The Opposite Direction."

My mother laughed. "Let's just focus on ourselves for now," she said, then sighed, reminding us of the comfort we once had, and how we now had to rely on charitable aid.

Strangely, these impossible times made our togetherness all the more beautiful. A new intimacy formed among us—no blame, no complaints, no regret. Maybe because every minute of life is a whole life, one that cannot be taken for granted.

In the late afternoon, we gathered with my parents and grandfather in a patch of sand adorned with basil seedlings we'd brought from our home—a keepsake of who we are and where we belong. We talked about our family tree, recited the names of the martyred, counted the wounded—each by name, age, and story. We recalled our noble roots, recounting the deeds, convictions, and lives of those who enriched us. The children listened with rapt attention, then peppered us with questions.

"Sidi,* how did you fall in love with Sitti† when she's such a strong Egyptian and you're utterly helpless without her?" They giggled.

He recounted the story they'd heard countless times, and they listened as though it were the first time.

The evening's treat was biscuits from the food aid, which we

---

*Grandpa.

†Grandma.

dipped in tea brewed over firewood, flames that blazed one moment and guttered the next.

A silent tear fell from my father's eye, the smoke darkening his face. A smile parted his lips, as if to reassure us we'll be alright. He asked, "Who's fetching the firewood tomorrow?"

No one answered. Instead, we all fled to sleep before the task could be assigned. We fell asleep before the night crickets stirred.

We awoke to the soft crackle of an old radio, its cord stretched from the shack's post to my father's wrist. The good news today: the price of eggs had dropped—eight for ten shekels. My mother announced that lunch would be shakshuka.

Everyone loved shakshuka—except me. I used to pick at the eggs and green peppers, leaving the tomatoes untouched. But hunger changed everything. Now I eat it with eager appetite. My family had long grown accustomed to my tiresome picky eating. In the past, my mother would prepare different dishes to suit our varying tastes. But now we all eat anything and everything, from the same plate, with a shared joy and grace.

At night, our sleeping space was shared too. My parents slept on a mattress. Ayah, the youngest and darling of the family, slept on another. The rest of us stretched out side by side atop heavy winter blankets that trapped our body heat.

We made it work. We endured the hardship. Being together softened our fear, maybe even kept it at bay altogether. My father stayed awake throughout the night, watching over us. He only slept by day, a habit he'd developed since our first displacement to Rafah. He couldn't bear to rest while his family faced the threat of death in the dark.

Sometimes I wondered if I would be as good a father as he one day.

In time, we even began to laugh at the absurdities of life in tents and shacks. The shared clothes, for one. We had all lost so much weight that we now wore the same size. Our few garments fit everyone. No one gained weight anymore, but love had grown—wider, deeper.

Tomorrow will come, and the same routines will repeat.

As the saying goes, "Halima will go back to her old ways." My mother will assign our tasks: Who will fetch the water? Who will stand in the breadline? Who will gather the firewood?

The Decision

By Khadija Abu-Lebdeh

Another night in that winter that made no distinction between house and tent. The buzz of the drones, unrelenting, throb in my head. My thoughts were tangled with the bed, scattered chaotically over it. My ears pick up the sound of the rockets, the artillery guns, and the roar of the sea. I trace the scraps of notes stuck to the headboard, its wooden fibers swollen with the dampness of this asbestos house. Our roof had cracked under the impact of shrapnel when our neighbor's cement house was bombed. The roof still held, but not without wounds—breaks and cracks that formed shapes, inviting the imagination to roam.

My eyes linger on the scribbles and the welter of lines my brother Qasim had drawn on the headboard. It's astonishing what a hand and pen can confess—an artist's thoughts and feelings rendered in indecipherable sketches and forms.

A purple blotch marks the time I tried to hide his drawings. Instead, it formed a pale lilac haze, like a transparent veil that made his drawing look surreal. I can still hear Qasim's shouts and protests that I had "ruined" his art. Mischief was my only skill back then—I didn't know that the tangled lines and entwined curves forming what looked like a flying horse, his mane streaming behind him and his tail struggling to catch up, was, indeed, a kind of art.

I was a menace when it came to that bed—securing one back

then was like winning the Nobel Prize. I was envious because I didn't have one. By day—when he wasn't home—I would claim it as mine, leading to war between Qasim and me, which always ended with my mother scolding me.

My purple handprints, a futile attempt to establish my ownership, had left strange shapes. The bed's thick legs looked as if they were standing with difficulty, like a man suddenly aged by war, on the verge of collapse. The bed was musty. The smell worsened as rain seeped through the walls, still upright with something like pride, having escaped the shelling up until then.

I sat cross-legged on the bed, my head churning with thoughts, as I tried to translate Qasim's scribbles into words. The pen fell from my hand at the voice of my older brother Ahmad, who came up to me, his face cheerful, though it carried news he knew I would not welcome.

"Ghada, my dear sister," he said gently. "I know what this bed means to you. How could I not. I've seen how you've clung to it since Qasim died."

I immediately knew what was coming next. The cylinder of cooking gas would not come soon, and we had already burned everything we owned as fuel. Now, he would ask for the bed. *Oh God, do not let him ask that!* I would not be able to object, in this hopeless situation. My lips trembled with a quiet gasp.

Ahmad continued, "I still remember it like it was yesterday—how you sat beside Qasim, whispering his name, holding his hand, trying to will him to live, until he drew his last breath. How you stayed on this bed through the whole mourning period. How you refused to let anyone sell it. But things are beyond my control, Sister. This pain has ravaged us—who knows pain better than us, who've lost mother and father in this season of mass killing, only to watch our brother devoured by illness?"

Ahmad paused, his eyes pleading, broken.

He's going to ask for it, I thought. *Please, my brother. Read my eyes. I can't give it up. Don't say it.* I screamed inside, but he said it:

"You know the heavy burden on me. I can barely get us food. There's nothing left to burn for fuel . . . except this bed."

"How can I give it up? Isn't there any other way?"

"You know I would never ask you for this if I had any other choice." His eyebrows pinched. His voice cracked and gave way to a heavy sigh. "I can't bear it anymore! What do you want me to do? Should I burn myself? . . . I'm tired, Sister. Try to understand how it breaks my heart to do this."

I said nothing. I knew how dire our situation was. But to let go of Qasim . . . the bed was the last trace of us together. I looked at Ahmad. Words failed me. No language could express the void beginning to swallow me.

The wooden frame creaked under me, and the thin walls seemed to lean in.

Ahmad felt my turmoil. "I won't pressure you anymore if you can't part with it. But think about it. Are memories of our departed loved ones more important than those still living?"

His words sank into me. Silence went on devouring my feelings, before they finally rebelled, and I pushed myself forcefully out of the void just before I hit the bottom. *How could Ahmad ask me to give up the bed?* I know reality is cruel. But this decision was crueler. *Why must we always give up our things? Is it for the sake of a life that might not be destined for us? Why can't I be selfish in my grief?* I screamed in silence and hurled myself onto the bed, carrying everything that could be broken, including my spirit, and burrowed into it in a silence weighed down by my thoughts.

I reached for the fallen pen. The bed wasn't made of fine oak or beech—just plain, old wood that bore priceless memories. I wrote a few thoughts and stuck them to the headboard:

Are memories of our departed loved ones more important than those still living?

Is there a way to earn money during a genocide without killing something inside us?

To die on a sickbed is a luxury. At least there's a bed.

The fire will not destroy the wood alone. I hear it. I hear the crackling of my own body.

My scattered thoughts kicked off the covers until dawn broke. I began gathering the sheets and cover from the bed. I stared at it long, committing every painful detail to memory. My vision blurred.

I read over the notes I'd stuck to it, as if it were my legacy. Then I sat before the fire, watching it devour Qasim's scribbles and strange patterns, mourning him all over again.

I wore a black sweater, watching the gray smoke curl to the sky. A tender breeze comforted me in a familiar way, lifting the smoke to wrap its warmth around me. The scent of the wood was unfamiliar. I closed my eyes to focus, imagining the fires carried Qasim's scent. For a moment, I lived in a beautiful illusion, as if I were in his arms, inhaling his scent, leaning into his warm chest. I opened my eyes, full of longing to see him. I reached out to touch him, enchanted by the flames lighting up his face. But the fire suddenly surged, pushing the cloud of smoke toward me with force. I choked and retreated, coughing. The firestorm rose like laughter, mocking the mirage that held me. The smoke rose again, veiled in black.

I pulled my hand back slowly, pressing my chest in slow circles, trying to dispel the trance that had overcome me. My lips parted involuntarily in a smile when I imagined Qasim's laughter mingling with the crackle of burning wood. *I wonder, was the bed a prison I put him in, or was it a prison for me?*

The flames licked at the scraps of notes pasted to the bed,

consuming their words letter by letter—first a blazing blue flame, then bright orange, glowing with colors of fire.

One charred fragment escaped the blaze. It floated lightly through the air before landing in my lap. It bore just two words, untouched by the fire:

the living

Delirium

By Amrou Al Najar

Every night, it's either a tense silence or the deafening voice inside your own head. Both flood your mind—a mind no longer able to think, imagine, or accept anything at all. Your heart begins to pound, you're seized by the loss of freedom. The loss of hope, loss of passion, loss of tenderness, loss of safety. Even going to the bathroom—small, putrid, dark, and suffocating—becomes a source of terror.

There's a crushing weight pressing down on my back. I cannot describe the pain. I'm lost, talking to myself, stunned by the enormity of what stirs in me. I want to write about everything, to speak about everything, but I don't know where to begin. What should I write about? About this second Nakba?* Or is it the third? I've lost track. Can a future truly exist after this genocide? Will there be life afterward? Is there a death deeper than the one crouching over us?

The beautiful things lived before all of this—tender adoration for our newly built home: My father's house, with its exquisite architectural details that reflected his attention and care for the smallest details. My mother's voice, near and far, present in every corner of the house. My father's arrival home and the loving

*"Nakba" means catastrophe, and it specifically refers to the 1948 Zionist expulsion of 80% of Palestine's Indigenous population from their homes and lands.

clamor that came with it—the sound of the door opening, his footsteps echoing as his shoes, always polished, tapped across the clean tiles. My brothers, one of them glued to a football match, cheering for his favorite team; my sister in her room, applying kohl skillfully to accentuate her wide eyes, rubbing earth-tone skin creams on her face, as sunlight filtered into every corner in the house, lighting up her honey-colored eyes and blooming life all around her.

Vibrant flowers in pots and basins suffused the house with their scent. The breezes stirred my spirit and fluttered the curtains with every gentle gust. I raised the volume on the radio, the better to hear Umm Kulthum sing "Amal Hayati," while I sipped from coffee whose aroma has wrapped the whole house in comfort, filling me with a sense that all is well in the world and everything is as it should be. Pebbles and seashells adorned the edges of the garden. The old wooden bench, worn by wind and sun, still endured, still strong. The towering palm trees whispered their commanding presence. Everything embraced me, until I grew tired of remembered love.

Yes, our home was a vast homeland, though it stood on just two dunums of land, inherited from my grandfather. It was nothing like the place we inhabit now. I often sat contemplating it, wondering how this "residence," a tiny space in a vast world, could evoke such enormous, constantly renewed love. There was harmony in its stones, colors, furniture, and design that spoke to the heart.

How could something newly built hold my uncle, who had only just returned after 45 years of exile, also be his final home in the world. My uncle never wanted to leave the house or its courtyard, because he had all he wanted there.

I was always proud of that house. Our house. It was big enough for the world and all its people. It held all of our family occasions, all of our stories: engagement parties for my cousins, tearful farewells and joyful reunions, feasts with friends and relatives, heated discussions, futile arguments, and intimate family evenings that meandered in laughter and contentment.

Ugh, how my soul aches!

I can't go on writing, even though my mind is teeming with thoughts and memories.

I feel scattered, broken, weak.

Visits to my aunt's house flicker behind my eyes—trips that renewed family ties. They are gone, forever. Gone in the blink of an eye—my father's sisters, their children and grandchildren, vanished, buried under the rubble.

We weren't there to embrace them in their final moments. We still haven't buried them. We can't. I sometimes wonder what their last thoughts were. Did they sense death approaching? Were they afraid? Were they all martyred at once? Or did one of them wave for help, waiting for someone who never came?

My aunt's cheerful husband and his two daughters, Salma and Laila, were crushed beneath a nine-story building. Their souls rose to the angels. But how did they bear such a death? I'm convinced that they didn't die instantly. Did they see their death staring at them? Did they feel it grip them? They always smelled so lovely. Did their sweet scent change when mixed with dirt, gunpowder, and blood? Will it become fragrant in martyrdom, or will you need a mask to shield you from the stench of decay? How will they be when worms begin their work?

Salma and Laila had clung to a single thread of hope, waiting to be pulled from the wreckage. All they'd ever known was art and music. Their fingers were the friends of melody and paintbrushes that sent love letters and love songs to those who knew them.

I imagine them crying, wanting their mother, or anyone, to comfort their terror.

I want to cry—but there's no time for crying.

I remember our garden, once bustling with my cousins' jokes and laughter. They're gone too. Why did they go and leave me to face this immense silence alone?

I think of my friends, the ones who used to boast of their accomplishments, their dreams that reached for the sky. They loved to gather in our garden, an open space for their music, their songs, their big existential questions.

I remember one of them asking, "Imagine if we got martyred."

The answer came, "Martyrdom is an honor . . . but not yet. Let's at least live our dreams, build the world we fought for. After that, if it's written, then let us be martyred."

He went on: "We're not afraid. Just . . . not now."

But they were martyred—afraid and shaking. I will never forget my last conversation with them. I could feel their fingers trembling as they messaged me. I could hear their anxious heartbeats. I sensed their bodies shivering in the cold. They left without one last look, or even a hug to quiet their fear. They took my heart with them.

We had promised to stay together. To survive all this together. They gave me their word, and I believed it.

As I was writing, the moon emerged from the clouds, pouring its splendor through the window. My eyes shone—how beautiful it is! In the pitch-black of night, the moon lit my heart, despite the sorrow. How can something so small and distant—so fleeting it feels like magic or delusion—illuminate my dark days?

Things are quiet for now. People are sleeping. It's cold. But my mind will not rest.

I hear a voice, not far away. It's our neighbor Abu Yasir. He was listening to the radio and talking to himself:

"Looks like there's a truce! Yes! Maybe we can breathe for a bit."

A shiver of anticipation rushed through me; I sat upright, borrowing some of his joy.

Suddenly, the radio fell silent. Abu Yasir's voice stopped. After a few moments, I heard him mutter, "Damnit! The battery's dead."

He switched everything off and went to bed, grumbling curses against the world.

I fell asleep late, my tears meeting the pillow before me, and I woke up early.

• • •

For me, coffee is the most powerful alarm—its aroma rouses and stirs me. My father prepares it with care and eagerness, even though it has become too expensive for most to afford. But my father is in a passionate love affair with his coffee. He would never betray it. And I—I cannot go without its call each morning, no matter the cost.

He brews it while humming Fairuz's song:

We're returning, O Love
Returning, O flower of the poor

His voice aches with longing to return to his home. He reminds me of the old days, before all this. I wonder, will he ever go back to that house? Will we ever gather around one table again, trading stories and gossip over a light supper he'd prepared with his kind touch?

The allure of coffee pulls me to my feet. My father is smiling as he hands me a cup, its aroma enfolding me.

The stillness was deceptive, shattered now by the sounds of cars and carts, shouting water sellers, and passersby cursing out loud, just as they curse silently inside. Children cry, not knowing in what land they will live or die.

But there's no harm in their making kites. With enthusiasm and excitement. Maybe it'll be a distraction.

The contrast between the quiet of coffee and the chaos of the street is jarring.

I braced myself for another day—for a fresh round of battles with myself, with people, with the streets, with the blazing sun—to get flour, drinking water, and food.

I left my tent wearing the same damned clothes that remind me every day of this Nakba. I walked with heavy, mournful steps through people, dusty cars, and a searing sun, asking myself:

How can the earth carry this much grief? This much sadness, crushing and cursed heaviness?

Where's the road? I'm lost.

Fashionista

By Fatma Asfour

Bodies, worn down by fear and exhaustion, sprawled across the floor of the eleventh-grade classroom at Mustafa Hafiz School in Khan Younis. At their center lay the tall figure of Rosa, arms outstretched as she woke from a long, difficult sleep, filled with pale images and voices of the past. She yawned and stretched, only to find strange faces at her feet and children nested by her arms. Women's bodies pressed together, heads resting by feet—dirty feet, for lack of water. The women were curled in on themselves to economize space. More than a hundred women had sought refuge in that room—toddlers, girls, women, and the elderly, a kaleidoscope of emotions, tempers, and unraveling nerves.

Most of the time, Rosa didn't remove her Tiffany prayer wrap. Her Gucci sandals had become tattered scraps that everyone in the classroom, women and children, took turns wearing to the latrine—a foul-smelling swamp overflowing with waste. A line of at least fifty people stood waiting to relieve themselves or to bathe (though it was rare to have enough water for that). Sometimes shouts and curses surged up and down the queue.

In this atmosphere, it was also common to hear laughter ringing from women huddled in corners—sharing whispers and raunchy jokes. Children spent their long wait playing and prancing around their mothers, who were quick to anger with them and with everything else.

Every other day, whistles and celebratory trills would erupt throughout the school-shelter, signifying the arrival of water, like they'd discovered a treasure. Men, women, and children would scramble with containers to collect their share before the tap ran dry again.

Rosa had two two-liter bottles that she filled whenever she could, using them to bathe and wash the jeans and crumpled white blouse she had fled in at the beginning of Israel's assault. She'd been wearing the same clothes for a whole month, washing them every two days and putting them back on wet, her body freezing in the winter cold.

One day, as a missile struck a nearby house, Rosa began to cry—her shrieks loud in the classroom, louder than the blast.

Everyone turned to stare as she screamed, "This is not my life! This is not me!"

She couldn't fathom how a fashionista, a designer, a creative soul like her had ended up in this squalid reality. Her hands trembled, and she beat the ground, as if striking back at fate. And just as quickly, she pulled herself together again.

When the call to the Asr prayer rang out, she stood to pray, seek God's forgiveness, and draw closer to Him in love and reverence. Just then her phone buzzed. The internet was back after a weeklong outage. She rushed to grab her phone, smiling.

"Finally! The internet is back!"

She scrolled through her Snapchat, Instagram, and the rest. She watched the outside world of dancing, outings, and simple fun, imagining herself returned to this normal life, or something like it.

She listened to some songs. Her slender waist and hips swayed instinctively. She danced in the middle of the classroom—a small rebellion to dispel the negative energy surrounding her. The women and children clapped to her rhythm, and for a moment she was a Disney princess.

She sat down after shaking her hips had helped lessen the effects of the rockets shaking the ground. Scrolling through Instagram, she came across a post in English from her cousin Wasim in Holland. Both his uncle's house—her home—and his grandfather's house had been completely destroyed. There was a photo of the wreckage, stones, broken columns, and a four-story apartment building reduced to nothing.

Rosa recognized remnants of her home in the rubble. "They bombed our house! It's gone! I can't see anything but rubble!" she cried out.

She stared at the photo, searching it for her bedroom, hoping to find signs that her clothes, jewelry, shoes, and handbags—especially the ones she'd brought from Saudi Arabia a month before Israel's assault—were safe. But she couldn't even locate her room. All the features of her house had disappeared.

Rosa had no sooner rid herself of some of the negative energy that was choking her than another avalanche of grief buried her again. She collapsed on the floor and slept. And didn't wake until dawn the next day.

"How about going to Abasan to check on our homes?" her sister Nesreen whispered to her.

Without thinking or considering the danger, she answered. "Yes!"

She washed her face, prayed the fajr, recited Qur'an and morning supplications, and made her personal prayer, entrusting herself and her possessions to God's protection. At 7:00 a.m., Rosa and Nesreen set out for Abasan al-Jadida—a place once a paradise, bursting with gardens, trees, and lovely houses. She donned a black abaya embroidered in blue and white, a white tarha over her head and neck, and sunglasses. It was a long way away, and she knew she was going to a forbidden zone, the "Death Zone." But she had to see.

All along the way, Rosa prayed fervently, her heart beating with the hope that she might salvage some of her clothing and her things, even though she was not bringing a suitcase or anything to carry what she might find. Her emotions swung wildly between hope and dread, taking bold, confident steps, then a slow, trepid pace weighed by anxiety.

This confusing feeling, wavering between yes and no, exhausted her. After nearly two hours of terror, walking a long road lined by ruins on both sides, Rosa and Nesreen reached "beautiful" Abasan—no longer paradise, but a mountain of rubble.

The sisters stopped at a collapsed mosque, a pile of stones topped by a minaret. Rosa realized it was Al-Farouk Mosque, which once stood between her home and Nesreen's. They agreed to search separately, then meet at the mosque, or what remained of it.

At first Rosa was lost, disoriented, and unable to locate where her home had been. She measured steps, trying to recall the arrangement of the buildings. Finally, she found it. Her nose filled with a foul stench. A herd of goats had been bombed, and their corpses were decomposing.

She scanned the area for the mint, basil, and flowers that had been there—any breath of life to dispel the rotten smell. But it was all gone. Everything beautiful was gone. Her feet ached from the long, tiring walk. She could barely climb over the wreckage. The buzzing of an Israeli drone, that iron fly, was terrifying. There was no one in this forbidden zone but Rosa and Nesreen, inspecting their homes.

Her feet caked in dust, Rosa stepped into her home—or what was left of it. She pushed through debris and rocks toward her old bedroom. Gray cement dust lodged under her fingernails. The white walls of her room had collapsed to the ground, leaving it open to what used to be her neighbors' house.

A white dove perched calmly, unexpectedly, atop the ruins of her room.

She stood in the middle of what had been her sanctuary, unsure where to start. In the corner, jutting from the wreckage, was her jewelry box. She rushed over the rocks toward it, unmindful of the cuts on her feet. She hugged it tightly to her chest, hope renewed that she might find her clothes and things.

She began digging—left corner first, where her wardrobe had been. It had held not just her designer clothes and handbags (the top brands), but a number of her own drawings and paintings she'd made.

She lifted the first layer of heavy rocks. Her heart pounded. Her tender hands turned black with layers of grime. Her face dripped with sweat. Her eyes sparkled.

She found wooden boards, part of her wardrobe. She dug faster, her heart racing.

There they were—her clothes, still on their hangers under the rubble.

She let out a shout of glee, as loud as the drone overhead. Rosa didn't care. She was so happy now.

Her joy quickly dimmed, the smile turning to a frown of regret. She hadn't brought a bag to carry them back. Then she remembered the bags under her bed. She located the wall where her bed had stood and cleared away piles of rocks and broken wood until she found them, along with her shoes, all of them, under what was left of the bed.

"Oh God, how great You are! How merciful!" she whispered.

She packed clothes, shoes, accessories, and cosmetics, filling all four cases—two she pulled on, and two lighter ones she slung over her shoulders. Miraculously, her strength returned. Her body moved with purpose.

She found a bottle of water in the debris of the kitchen and used it to wash her hands and feet. Then an explosion erupted close by.

"They bombed Nesreen!" she screamed.

A voice shouted, "Rosa! Are you okay? Answer me!"

It was Nesreen.

Rosa ran to hug her, thanking God, and the fashionista set off confidently, her head high and her beautiful smile lighting up her face, carrying the bags with ease.

The sisters walked 2 kilometers, unable to find any transport, until they came across four young men from the neighborhood. They men were astonished—two women in Abasan, a declared death zone, hauling so many bags. They offered to carry the bags to Al-Alam Roundabout in Bani Suheila, the closest place to find any means of transport—a car, a truck, or even a donkey cart. Nesreen accompanied them, her load of "plunder" much lighter than her sister's, while Rosa borrowed a bicycle from one of the young men.

She flew on the bicycle, pedaling daringly ahead to their meeting point, the air of Abasan caressing her face. For that moment, Abasan was Beautiful Abasan again. No death falling from the sky or piled up in the roads. It was one of the most beautiful days of her life.

People stared at her—surprised, disapproving.

"Are we in a genocide, or what?" one muttered.

"Mashallah! Mashallah!" another exclaimed in admiration, while a third flirted jokingly, "Check out the babe on the bicycle!"

Rosa would wear what she loved again. She would wonder what to wear and choose her outfits. She would be beautiful again, a fashionista. She would be herself.

"This is me!" she shouted to the heavens, racing the wind.

For Gaza to Leave Us Something

By Nebal Al-Najjar

The seventh of October. Six in the morning. We were getting ready to harvest the olives. It was the season. A family tradition led by my grandmother. Olive picking is one of the most cherished times of the year, bringing us together with song and folk hymns, with tea, warm bread, and zaatar.

Our hands became crutches for our matriarch, who walked at the helm, her heart already racing ahead toward our land in the village of Khuza'a in Khan Younis. The land was lush, its soil fragrant with generous life. Its birds greeted us, a burst of color against a crystalline sky.

As we gathered our tools for the harvest, ready to walk and savor the day's beauty, the hour of damnation struck.

The morning, brimming with passion and anticipation, transformed into a cacophony of terrifying sounds that pierced our ears and exploded our minds. We stumbled in panic, desperate to understand what was happening.

Murmurs arrived quickly from neighbors. Gaza's fence had been breached. The resistance had reached the "Gaza envelope"*—but there was no official news, no clarity.

---

*The Israeli-controlled borderlands around the Gaza Strip—areas, in fact, that were part of Gaza according to the original 1948 armistice line, and where Israeli settlements are built atop Palestinian villages where many Palestinians in Gaza are from.

Hours passed. We saw with our own eyes what our minds could not comprehend.

Was this the Day of Judgment, or were we trapped in a collective nightmare? We found ourselves running—young and old alike—abandoning Khuza'a, our homes, and everything that held meaning, to save our lives. Images and scenes of the 1948 Nakba replayed before our eyes, but this time it was our Nakba. A real, living Nakba, vivid and raw—not an old, faded photo or a dim, black-and-white archival reel.

Our anguish raced ahead of us, and we walked chasing our tears, unable to fathom the world around us or where we were headed. We made it to a relative's home and paused to catch our breath. To rest a little.

As we arranged the few simple belongings we'd managed to carry in our flight, a deafening explosion thundered too close, sending us running for our lives once again. Adrenaline surged, hurling us to yet another place to hide. Again, we walked, our steps racing against the pounding in our chests, carrying broken bags full of our broken lives and broken dreams, trying to hold our children close, as they clung to our bodies.

Finally, we reached another stop in our exodus, gasping for breath to hold on. After we spent twenty days clinging to life by a thread, Israel issued an order to evacuate the area. Our third displacement in less than one month. Adrenaline, that primal instinct for survival, again fueled our flight to another haven—this time a school turned shelter for death deferred.

My heart boiled with fury when I saw men, women, and children bickering over a pot of rice. I wept a thousand tears.

The school-shelter was near Nasir Hospital, in the middle of Khan Younis. It buzzed with noise and throngs of displaced people, making days blur into night. And at night, we braced for death that could come at any moment. Ambulance sirens competed with speeding cars, their horns screaming desperate pleas to clear the roads. They carried the wounded—women, children, and men with severed limbs—or the dead, the fortunate ones whole, or body parts of unknown identity.

Our nights were spent trembling; fear spread like a plague. Whispers of the shahada* murmured around us, each of us convinced the day would be our last.

At the time, I did not realize how blessed I was, until I went to the injury ward, seeking a water source to make ablutions for the Maghrib prayer. I saw a man crushed by grief, like a piece of his heart had been cut out. His four-year-old daughter lay unconscious on a bare cot. He stared helplessly at her, his gaze empty and lost. His lips trembled as he whispered prayers, his fingers running over the beads of the masbaha.†

"I beg you, O Lord. Healing is from you, O God. You are lord of the weak and vulnerable, O God."

I wept too, though I wasn't sure why. Was I crying for the helpless father? Or the little girl robbed of her leg and arm by a hateful Israeli missile? She was beautiful, as children her age are, perhaps longing to wake up and play with her friends. I resisted the urge to stroke her hair, which was pooling around her small face. I imagined her mother combing it, weeping, assuring her she'd always be beautiful.

But in that moment, I also felt grateful. For the blessings of an unscathed body, at least for now.

I returned to our ignoble shelter, shattered by the scene. It kept replaying in my mind as I struggled to comfort my children, to provide them food, to meet their needs—responsibilities their

---

*Shahada is the Muslim declaration of faith and a core pillar of Islam. It is a statement of one's belief in the oneness of God and the acceptance of Muhammad as God's messenger. It is recited at the time of death as an affirmation of faith, a source of final peace, a final submission, and a key to God's paradise.

†Muslim prayer beads, similar to Christian rosary beads.

father would have shouldered. But he had left two weeks before that cursed day, traveling abroad for work to provide for us.

And so our days passed—three months of this bitterness. Then came our fourth displacement. We thought it would be the last time, a place where we could breathe. But I found myself in a tent with my children, their grandmother, and their uncle, surrounded by countless others like us, in a desolate, frightening wasteland.

Now, four months into the misery of this camp, I try to write, hoping words might ease the loss and grief carved on our hearts—the loss of people, home, places. The loss of Gaza, of the world we knew.

Thousands of stories. Thousands of cold houses, without their families. Thousands of empty embraces. All form the memory of a city grieving alone, suffering alone, and dying alone in this world.

I no longer want to be part of Gaza's calamity and of her inferno. Let her die alone.

But leave us something. A root. A green stem. A patch of green earth. A disobedient wind. An untamed sea. Water drawn from the well of memory. A naughty child laughing. A heart pounding with first love. And a future yet to come.

Gone

By Maram Hammou

A patchy darkness blanketed the camp, yet it bore no trace of stillness. No one was asleep. Faint lights flickered nervously from the tightly packed homes. That night, four families, including ours, huddled together through an extraordinary storm of bombs.

Fear held us in its grip. Deafeningly violent explosions never stopped, each one shaking the earth as if the sky itself might collapse.

The house rocked, and we heard stones, glass, and shrapnel crashing down, as though the missiles were raining directly on our heads. Then came the acrid stench of gunpowder and ash—of memories.

The tattered cloth we'd hung in place of a window—shattered in a previous blast—flapped wildly. We all crouched low. Children screamed—sometimes the adults too.

My heart pounded so fiercely I could hear it, even as every explosion deafened my ears. I lost count of how many times I squeezed my eyes shut, then opened them to make sure nothing had collapsed around me—that the scenes I'd lived through before had not repeated here.

I gathered myself, feigning strength, trying to calm the frightened souls around me. I told them the shelling was distant, that we must trust in God, the only protector.

Another explosion cut through my heart and made me tremble. This blast was different. It felt like it ripped out my soul. A bad omen. But as always, I brushed the feeling aside and tried to soothe those around me.

Dawn approached.

My father's phone rang, breaking the silence, filling our hearts with dread.

"Hello! Who? When? La hawla wala quwwata illa billah!"*

We watched my father, trying to read his face to make out what happened. His brief, stunned words told us that someone had been killed. Sorrow in the heart can be multiples of what the face shows, but my father's burrowed brow and the sweat streaming down his face told the whole story in a language more brutal than words ever could.

The call ended, after what seemed like an eternity. We waited for the details. Our eyes full of questions, our tongues tied, unable to ask, *Who?*

With halting words, a trembling voice, and eyes brimming with tears, he told us my aunt's house—full of our beloveds—had been bombed.

Shock scribbled on our faces, and time stopped. Trauma sat next to me, like a heavy shadow. My body crumbled, my tears dried up, and words were choked in my chest. Each time I tried to speak, the words retreated into an abyss of sorrow that tore at my soul. Unanswered questions wheeled in my head, pulling me down deep into a dark world.

Why did they kill my aunt?

Why did they steal her loving eyes from me?

Who will replace her embrace, she who was so proud of me in my moments of triumph?

How will I live without hearing her voice call my name?

---

*Literally translates to "There is no power or might save only with God." Muslims (and Arab Christians) utter this affirmation of God's omnipotence as a reassurance in times of great loss, injustice, and powerlessness.

Why did I have to lose the heart I loved so dearly?

My dearest aunt—my hope, my anchor and champion at every step, my support as a medical student. How she waited to see me graduate as a doctor!

She always believed in me, told me that I would be a force to be reckoned with in this world. With her violent death, I felt like I was burying my dreams along with her.

Her passing broke my heart. It shattered something inside me—something I cannot name or describe, but I felt it extinguish in my chest all at once, just like that.

Voices clamored around me—some asking for details, others trying to discern who exactly had been killed in the strike. Voices swelled, intertwining in confusion and panic, then gradually quieted, as if the truth were entering on tiptoe from the heavy silence. It was like an open grave swallowing the last fragments of peace and life.

I sat among the grief-stricken faces, scanning their grim expressions, wavering between shock, denial, and disbelief. I was alone, as alone as one could ever be. I felt like one struck senseless, waiting for the rest of the news to come. It never comes all at once. It arrives in waves of pain and grief, each one heavier than the last, breaking your back a little at a time.

My aunt was gone.

Her husband, her daughters, her sons, her grandchildren, her daughters-in-law, and her sons-in-law, her relatives—all gone.

Other kin were gone.

Our neighbors—gone.

Our home and everything in it were gone.

The neighborhood, its character, its people. Gone.

They're all gone.

The Cobbler

By Samya Al-Laham

The days melted and blended into each other. We could no longer discern the days of the week. News and events repeated and blurred into sameness—the massacres were all the same; the shouts and crying of children were all the same. Death never left this city. Death became our daily companion. And we became numb—indifferent to everything.

I was looking for a shoe repairman on my way back from the Culture and Free Thought Center, one of the few remaining safe spaces in Gaza, to the refuge where we'd been displaced. The heat was unbearable, sweat pouring from me in torrents.

I had to walk a long way before I finally found him—an elderly man, with a long gray beard and a tattered red cloth tied around his head. The lines on his face bore the weight not of age, but of sorrow and defeat. He sat on a wooden stool, stitching a shoe, surrounded by a small sea of worn-out sandals and broken shoes.

He hadn't been a cobbler before—not really—but the cruelty of war had obliged him to sit on this grim stool in this new role, to feed his family.

I approached him hesitantly.

"God give you strength," I said shyly. "Could you fix this shoe for me, please? You know how it is . . . there aren't any shoes left in the whole town."

Without lifting his head, he replied in a strained voice: "Of course. Don't worry. But you'll have to wait your turn."

I nodded. "Alright, I'll wait. But how much do you charge for it, Uncle?"

"A hundred shekels!" he teased.

I laughed, "I'm generous, and you're worth it. God's blessings upon you."

"May God reward and grant you success, Daughter."

I waited nearly half an hour, standing with the others in line, the sun beating down on our heads. The area was crowded with displaced people. Street vendors peddled their wares, shouting from every direction, and an ambulance siren rang out: "Make way! We have a critical case!"

When it was finally my turn, the wartime cobbler stitched the torn upper part of my shoe, securing it back to the sole. It didn't take him long, as thought he'd been doing this all his life.

He lifted his head and looked at me, his face darkened and burned by a merciless sun. His eyes, red and swollen like coals, brimmed with tears. His hands, aged and cracked, quivered with fatigue.

In a voice faltering with brokenness, he told me, "By God, Daughter, after my two eldest girls—my first joy—were killed and I lost my house . . . nothing matters to me anymore. Not money. Not possessions. Not even my own life."

Small tears fell down his face.

Something tore inside me. I couldn't stop my own tears—they fell freely from my eyes. I pulled myself together. "May God have mercy on them, Uncle," I said. "And may He reward you with goodness and heal your heart. May they someday be your intercessors with Him. And no matter what, Alhamdulillah."

He nodded, murmuring, "Alhamdulillah." I took the shoe and held out the money, but he demurred, saying, "No, dear . . . I don't want any money."

But I insisted: "No, by God! You've earned it, and you must take it"

Only after my insistence did he accept. I bade him farewell, trying to hold composure in front of him. "Don't be sad, Uncle," I said. "Nothing in this world lasts. We're all on the same path."

I walked away; my head bowed. I didn't want anyone to see me cry.

The Breadline

By Ali Abu-Zayed

It was a quiet night of genocide in the Gaza Strip. The clock showed 3:30 a.m. I was deep in sleep, something we'd been deprived of for many days since the war began, when my wife, heart of my heart, woke me in a hushed voice:

"Ali, Ali! Get up so you can get a place in line at the bakery. You can sleep when you get back. God give you strength!"

I looked at her and got out of bed, thinking to myself, *We can't even enjoy a night's rest anymore*. I went to the bathroom to wash and perform ablutions, but there was no water. I remembered that I'd not filled the tank because Abu Jamil, the water-truck man, hadn't come yesterday. The municipal water had been cut off from our area for some time because of a lack of fuel. I used a bottle of drinking water for the ablutions, got dressed, and walked to the bakery not far from our home.

Despite the relative calm, fear and caution clung to me. I quickened my pace to secure a good spot at the front of the breadline, hoping to return quickly to get the rest of my sleep.

The line was already full of people by the time I arrived. But I told myself, *It's okay, there aren't that many ahead of me. I'll wait for Hajj Dhiyab, the bakery owner, to arrive and distribute numbered tickets.*

The sky was clear, and the air was fairly warm. The men in line were talking about the state of things—what we had come to, our people's suffering, and the genocide that has swallowed us all. When the call to the dawn prayer rose into the air, I prayed right there in the street to keep my place in line, then returned to chatting with the guys.

There was a young man I hadn't seen before, a stranger in our neighborhood. He was tall, wheat-skinned, with long, wild hair, like it hadn't been cut in ages. His name was Faisal. He was talking about the misery of his displacement. He was from Gaza City, but the genocide forced him to flee south. He started telling me about the hardships he'd faced on his way down, and I was so absorbed in his story that I ignored the others around me.

Faisal recounted a horrific experience during his family's displacement, when they were stopped at the Hallaba*—a checkpoint the Israeli military had set up for fleeing Gazans. He spoke of the bitterness of what happened, "When it was my turn to cross, an Israeli soldier told me to move to the left. Everyone who was stopped there experienced every sort of humiliation, pain, and degradation. An Arabic-speaking soldier approached, demanding ID, then he ordered me to strip." Faisal fell silent, tears in his eyes.

I whispered, my skin crawling, "Did you take it all off?"

"Down to my boxers. Without hesitation. I knew any hesitation could cost me my life." He went on, his voice heavy with grief as he recalled the scene, "I took off my clothes piece by piece, trembling in fear."

The breadline had grown longer, and young men were jostling to secure a place. I avoided the pushing—Hajj Dhiyab hadn't yet arrived to distribute the numbered tickets. My attention stayed fixed on Faisal. He went on.

"The soldier tied my hands behind my back and blindfolded me as I kneeled. Then he left. I started thinking—what now? will they arrest me? kill me? let me go?" Faisal's face twisted, his voice cracked, and he swallowed hard before continuing. "I

*Hallaba means "the milker" or "milking station."

was mostly worried about my wife and child—he's not yet four. They'd crossed the Hallaba while I was detained. My wife is from Gaza City and didn't know anything about the southern area. I remained in the same kneeling position for what felt like forever. I couldn't move at all, terrified of meeting the same fate as others who'd been detained."

He paused, gathering his thoughts, "I don't know how much time passed while I was like that. Eventually, a soldier came and returned my ID, removed the blindfold, untied me, and ordered me to go south immediately. I grabbed my clothes and ran. Didn't look back, and crossed the entire distance nearly naked, in front of the crowds of displaced men, women, and children, before I could put on my clothes."

Faisal was careful to lower his voice when he was telling me about his nakedness. He cupped a hand over his mouth, afraid others would hear. He went on, "And that's when the search began for my wife and son. I pulled my phone from my pocket and tried to call her. No answer."

In the meantime, Hajj Dhiyab had arrived and begun distributing numbered tickets to lessen the chaos in the line. I had been waiting for hours. I took my number and went back to Faisal, still tuned to his story.

Then. Suddenly. An explosion.

The blast was thunderous, swallowing the place. Screams rose one after the other—"Medic! Help!" We didn't know where they came from. The sky was covered with dust. We couldn't see anything.

When at last the cloud of dust and smoke began to settle, we looked around for each other in panic. People ran wildly, calling out for their sons and brothers who'd been in the breadline—most of them young men, boys, children. A distant siren grew louder. I tried to gather my senses, to comprehend what had just happened.

It turned out that the Israeli annihilation planes had struck a house next to the bakery.

My wife came running, searching for me. She pulled me into her arms. I was covered head to toe in dust. I could hear her heart pounding in terror as she wiped the grime from my face with her warm hands.

"Thank God you're safe, my love," she said. "Come on, let's go home. Forget the bread!"

My eyes scanned the faces around me, all of them powdered in ash. I was looking for Faisal. I don't think he had finished telling his story.

Umbilical Cord

By Maysa Salama

In these barren times, separation and reunion embrace in anguish, and the smell of dust chokes the breath of waiting. The terrifying blast of shelling and the crash of collapsing buildings echo on the horizon.

The crowd thickens. He grips her hand like a song stifled by the road, pulling their mischievous daughter close to keep her from slipping away. He hears only what his eyes see—fear and fragments of stolen speech—words he lip-reads, trying to decipher the chaos around him.

A soldier's grating voice calls out: "Women and children forward! Men fall back!"

Night descends inside her chest. She weeps, looks to her husband, then hands him their swaddled newborn to free her hands. With trembling fingers, she translates the soldier's command into sign language.

He tracks the language of her hands, his gaze swelling with tenderness. In the midst of the moving throng, he sees only her—her honey-colored eyes glistening with tears, and her radiant, youthful face aged overnight. Her eyelids fall, and she leans toward him, sobbing, leaning all her weight into these last moments with him.

This, then, is the moment of parting.

He returns their newborn to her, sweat dripping from his face. He removes the backpack of essentials he'd carried through the grueling journey—diapers, clothes, basic hygiene items, and the family identification papers. Gently, he helps secure it on her back, overwhelmed by a heavy sense of helplessness. He can no longer be her support, her pillar and chest to lean on. He is powerless to ease her burden, to protect her or their children.

With hands that tremble and collide, he tells her, "You must go forward—be brave! I don't want to lose you or the girls. Be strong! Go now!"

Through a veil of tears, she listens to his hands and screams silently. *How can I leave you alone? No one knows you can't hear—and your hearing aid isn't with you. I just can't; if I have to die, let me die loving you. What good is life if you're not in it?*

He keeps urging her, pleading. Finally, under the crushing weight of his love and the need to save herself and their daughters, she relents—her face weary, her heart like a dried walnut.

He pulls a pen from his pocket and writes the name of their eldest, Mestika, on her hand. Then he ties her wrist to their daughter's with a rope, as though fashioning a new umbilical cord that might deliver her safely into the world once more, three years after her birth—so she wouldn't get lost or swallowed into the belly of this nightmare.

She cries bitterly. He wraps them in his arms, the three becoming music in his embrace. To keep his own tears at bay, he signs to her with his eyes and his hands, "Feed me with the bread of your smile. I'm hungry, darling. I love you. I have faith in you."

Standing like a broken shadow, he bends to kiss Mestika. "My love, I tied your hand to Mama's so you don't fly away, little butterfly," he said. "Take care of her."

She walks slowly away, her steps heavy. She has left her heart behind. She is overcome with terror, dragging her little one by that new umbilical cord, clutching the baby to her chest, as death circles overhead like a vulture, its stench in every breath.

She pushes forward, melting into the throng of bodies, amid

the threats from arrogant soldiers and her fear of losing Mestika beneath the stampede.

The cord tightens painfully around Mestika's small wrist with every tug. The baby screams at her chest, as if calling out cries of death, only a few days after her first cry of her life. She shifts her a little to the left, over her heart, but her crying becomes sharper. She looks at her tearfully, helpless, unable to nurse her. Her insides churn.

"I know you're hungry, my little one," she whispers apologetically. "But there's nothing to be done."

Mestika is crying too. Her mother's nerves unravel from their cries.

They reach the first checkpoint—what they ironically call the Hallaba. The weight of her backpack is cutting her in two, the pressure threatening to pour afterbirth down between her legs. *Has it already?* She wonders if its red color already trails her.

A soldier yells, ordering the women to sit on the ground, arms raised. The ground shrinks beneath her. She glances around. Tears flood every eye. Anxious anticipation rules the air. Humiliation and cursing echo. The women sit silently like coffins, waiting to cross.

Minutes later, a damned soldier orders them again to their feet. She gathers her strength to stand, pulling on the cord. She touches her belly, still marked by childbirth, and smooths down her clothes, embarrassed.

Again, the soldier barks, "Hold up your IDs!"

She raises her ID in the hand tied to Mestika, squeezing her daughter's wrist.

Oh God, why must we die so many times before we finally die? Must our lives exist at the mercy of the fleeting whims of a fleeting soldier?

Mestika tugs the down on the cord, crying.

"Mama, I won't fly away! Don't pull so hard—it hurts!" she

protests. “Where’s Baba? Can he carry me? I don’t want the rope.”

Mestika’s words claw at her chest. She swallows hard, as if a stone lodged in her throat. She pulls the cord gently, drawing her daughter close. Her whole body trembles. *What do my daughters have to do with this madness? Why are we the only people forced to give our children life at life’s end?*

Calls of alarm ripple through the crowd. She stands as if before an executioner. Then the soldier finally allows them to cross. She examines the red stains and the cord. The baby is still crying.

She feels faint, pushing forward among the other women and children. There’s no difference now between a terrified little girl and an old woman etched with frailty.

She tries to hold on, but she faints.

She opens her eyes to a circle of women around her, trying to revive her.

“My daughters!” she shouts.

A woman places the baby in her arms. She cradles her close, inhaling her milky smell—the scent of contentment. Mestika flutters around her at the end of the cord, like a sunflower spinning in orbit. She leaps into her mother’s lap.

“Mama, you were going to fly away if I hadn’t held on to you,” Mestika announces. “I’ll tell Baba I saved you.”

An elderly lady, herself crying, gives her a few drops of water.

“Daughter, we are all losers in this game of death. The lucky ones are those who survive with the least loss,” the old woman says. “I left my children behind, my provision for time to come and my crutch for old age. But God’s mercy prevails. Now get up and nurse your baby.”

The old woman’s words soothe her heart. She rises to find a bit of cover to nurse her infant daughter. As she stands, the smell of her own blood on the ground and on her clothes bring more tears than before.

She holds her baby close as she sits to nurse her beside the shell of a bombed-out cart, thinking about her husband: *What's happened to him? What if they speak to him and he can't answer? What if they shoot him?*

Questions swarm in her head. *Who will explain to a ruthless soldier that her husband cannot hear? That he's lost his hearing aids—the little device that buzzed in his head with the frequencies of their drones? Will his fate be prison? Torture? Death?*

The enemy has plunged him into an ocean of silence that is not at all silent.

But love is strong, like death.

The Story Isn't Over

By Samah Abu-Awwad

I stepped into a school-shelter. It was already filled with crowds of displaced people—all fleeing terror, clinging to the hope that schools would be safer. I glanced to my left, then right, scanning every corner for a spot—any small opening that would be enough to hold me and my meager belongings.

Children screamed in panic. Some were searching for the last of their family members. A woman sobbed for her lost son. Men, some elderly, had claimed whatever space was left, their faces drawn tight, despondent.

I kept searching for a space to rest. The schoolrooms were packed. The hallways swarmed with children—some were playing; others sat in silence. Their faces bore no resemblance to childhood.

I entered a classroom full of women and children, and a cacophony of shouting and crying. Suitcases and scattered belongings filled every corner. I glimpsed a small patch of floor in the middle of the classroom, left empty as an aisle.

I took it immediately, sat on the floor with my bags, waiting for my heartbeat to calm. The space was barely a square meter, so small and confining. I crouched into myself to fit, scanning the room for a familiar face. They were all strangers, but all of us carried the same weight.

I began to feel suffocated, short of breath and needing air. I rushed to a window, closed my eyes, and inhaled deeply. Instead of oxygen, my lungs filled with dust still lingering from the shelling that made me cough. I returned to my little spot, searching through my bag for a sip of water.

The noise of children woke me early the next day—some playing, others crying. Women were chatting. In the hallway outside, men exchanged the latest news. My head throbbed with pain, and I struggled to my feet to find water to wash my face, hoping to summon enough energy to stand in the food-aid line—for a meal that would not satisfy hunger. *But as the saying goes, Better the whiff of stew than none at all.*

I stood waiting in the long line. A fight broke out between two women quarreling over their place in line. My turn finally came after endless hours of waiting—my body and feelings numb. I received a food ration: one can of cheese and a can of fava beans. Nothing else.

I walked away from that corner of collective misery, trying to convince myself, *This isn't real life. This isn't our reality.*

The day dragged on, slow and heavy, until night fell, which brought suffering of another kind. The basic question that tormented the displaced was: *How shall we sleep?* Followed by another: *Where shall we place our bedding?*

I wasn't thinking about how and where. I just curled into myself, worn down by exhaustion, tired from loss—the loss of lives, of home, of dreams, of the past and present—and of what might still come.

There was a brief moment of stillness in the universe—a fleeting silence between two air strikes, amid the hush of sleeping, drained bodies. It was a moment when my faraway dreams flickered to life. It felt so real. I drifted off with that lovely feeling—sure that I would wake up at home, surrounded by the things I love, by my family, my life, my memories, and the stories I would one day write.

For the Sake of Diapers

By Abdallah Al-Sayyed

A street vendor called at the top of his lungs: "Pampers! A bag for 240 shekels!"

For the fifth time, I scoured the market for baby diapers at a price my dwindling income—eroded by Israel's aggression—could bear. I'd spared no effort, knocking on every door, from aid organizations to UNRWA, seeking diapers and baby formula. Each attempt chipped away at my dignity, my spirit hollowed by my inability to secure the barest necessities of life.

Yesterday, a woman I know called me, her voice trembling with shame. She knew I worked with local aid organizations. She explained her difficult circumstances and swallowed her pride to ask if I could get diapers for her child. Her words struck me harder than the buzz of the Israeli drone in the background, interwoven with her baby's cries that seemed to shake the heavens.

After a week without a signal, I finally reached Howaida, an activist who works with a foundation that provides support of this kind.

"Hello, Howaida. How are you holding up? I hope you're well."

"Alhamdulillah, we're still alive! Surviving. As you know, everything's hard."

"May God help us all. I'm calling about something important, and I know you're the right person to ask. I need diapers—urgently."

"Supplies are tight," she said, "but we'll add the baby's name to the list. Inshallah, it will work out. Come by tomorrow morning; don't worry."

This genocidal war has turned my life into a bitter, relentless battle to secure basic essentials, always on the run, dodging death from one place to another. Unlike my previous self, I've grown restless, eager to leave the house early—a change so stark everyone noticed. They didn't understand, as if I were rushing toward my death.

My wife, Amal, didn't want me to go. It was nearly 8:00 a.m. She begged me to wait an hour or two, at least until the streets filled, believing the bustle was the safest time, when air strikes briefly slowed. She tried tugging at my heartstrings with tender looks, hoping to sway my emotions and get her way—she knew I couldn't refuse her. When that didn't work, she pretended to be unwell, insisting she needed me at her side. Her attempts failed, but I reassured her that I was simply going to check on my mother, who had been displaced from her home and was living at my sister's house nearby. She knew that would keep me off the streets until at least ten, which is what she wanted in the first place.

At this, she bid me goodbye, urging me to be careful "Stick to crowded streets, my love. It's safer," she said, more to convince herself than me.

Fleeing death from place to place changed me. I've become a homebody, fixated on improving the details of our survival to endure this ordeal. I've become more afraid. This Israeli aggression has been unlike the previous one. It's extermination, collective punishment. When I walk through the streets now, I see the hollowed faces of my people, and I feel the weight of their empty pockets at every stall. We are all the same now. You can look at someone and tell, just by their clothes, how much they had lost, how this genocidal war has eroded them—and how it has eroded you too.

At about 8:20 a.m., I knocked on my sister Nehad's door.

"What's wrong? Why are you here so early?" she fired off questions before I could slip off my shoes. Worry and fear contorted her face—perhaps she was expecting me to announce a family member's injury or death, or that a home had been bombed. In times like these, no one expects good news, especially not this early in the day; they expect only the worst news under this relentless genocide.

My mother beamed upon seeing me, and it filled me with a quiet happiness. Imagine a mother's longing gaze, reunited with her son after too long apart. Her embrace nearly crushed my ribs. I'd missed her terribly. I missed the way she traced the contours of my face with her fingertips, smiling so wide it strained her cheeks.

And yet, her tenderness was laced with something else. Her eyes brimmed with fear and unuttered questions. I answered before she asked.

"I left early to get diapers for a child whose mother had turned to me in desperation," I said. "They're from the north. Displaced to a tent in Khan Younis." I explained that they had left with nothing but the clothes on their backs. Her husband, a day laborer, had lost all income and could barely provide bread. But all they wanted were diapers for their baby.

I knew my mother's heart. The suffering of others weakened her. She encouraged me to help, but not at the cost of my safety.

"Don't put yourself in danger," she warned.

She insisted I have tea and eat something—bread with duqqa and tomatoes—to fend off a headache. My mother knows me well. She senses what I need without a word from me.

My visit was brief. Unlike in normal times, when I'd spend hours with her, we rushed through conversations in a matter of minutes. I had to be on my way, hoping to bring the family a bit of joy by securing diapers.

As I left, my mother offered directions. "Avoid that street—it's near a threatened house. Take the other one!" She pointed toward a road that didn't lead to my destination. Her sense of direction had slipped. In a rush, I put on my shoes by the door and gulped the tea she'd poured into a paper cup for me.

My mother's face, laden with worry, followed me like a trembling shadow.

What if the street I'm walking on is bombed?

I stopped, trying to recall her advice, to discern the "other street" she meant.

What if I took the wrong path?

I imagined my mother panicked, Amal weeping. I quickened my pace. But questions hounded me, heavy with foreboding.

Amal, who refuses to hear my last will and testament, who argues with me and cries at any talk of my passing—will she carry out my final wishes?

What shape will their heartache and grief take?

What will my child Hamza look like grown up?

What will his life be like?

Will he remember me?

Will he recall the moments we shared as father and son, and the many times I forgave his mischief, won over by his wit and charm?

Then, a more terrifying question, one I tried to silence: *Would Hamza even live to grow up?*

In that moment, all my fears and haunting thoughts were swept away by a far greater terror falling from Gaza's sky, raining death. A missile struck. The explosion's roar transcended sound itself. Its impact with the earth shook me to the core and tore apart the images of my mother, Amal, and Hamza that crowded my mind.

I was shocked to see a young man fall in front of me. Torn between instinct and conscience—to run and save myself, or try to help him—I chose survival. As I turned to find cover, a second missile struck, less than a minute after the first. The blast lifted and hurled me, slamming my body to the ground about 4 meters away.

My clothes were torn, my leg burned, and blood seeped into my shoes. But I forced myself to keep moving, limping toward safety. One thought took hold of me, more than my wounds: *My mother. She heard the blast.*

Ignoring the pain, I dragged myself toward my sister's home. My breath was ragged, my vision hazy. Dust clung to my hair and skin. My pants were shredded, my foot soaked in blood.

I finally reached the door and could hear her voice, soft, pained, and heart-wrenching. My mother is calling my name, "Abdallah, Abdallah." I can hear the terror in her voice.

I mustered what reserves of strength I had and opened the door, raising my hands and spinning slowly to reassure her that I was okay. I took a few steps, leaning on my pride alone, for my foot, my knee, and my stomach screamed in pain.

More than anything, I wanted to collapse in my mother's arms and weep like a child. But I couldn't. Because that would worsen her anxiety and break her heart to see me defeated like that.

So I chose silence.

And I don't know for how long I can keep choosing silence.

From Tent to Tent

By Lubna Meqdad

On the sixty-seventh day of the genocide, we fled our family home in Hamad City to a patch of farmland in Mawasi, Khan Younis, where dozens of displacement tents had sprung up, planted like grief in the soil.

We settled in a tent built by members of our extended family—my uncle and his sons—using white nylon sheeting and wood planks. It had two sections. The men's area contained an old, worn rug for sleeping, a wooden table holding kitchen and cooking wares, a gas burner beside it, and, beneath the table, some canned foods—rations we were forced to purchase, even though they were supposed to be distributed for free to displaced families like us.

The women's side is where we slept on a straw mat with a few blankets. There were sacks of flour we'd bought at exorbitant prices, after two months of Israel's siege without even a handful of flour available in the markets.

Dividing the two sections hung a tattered blanket, a flimsy partition between the men and women.

To the back of the tent, a wall enclosed the farm. We placed a few possessions there, things we'd salvaged from our house—now only a memory. We women shared our bedding with the children for warmth. My pillow was the coat I wore everywhere. My fingers were cracked from the cold, my hands were rough and weary from forced displacement, and my head pounded from the ceaseless buzzing of drones overhead. When I finally collapsed at the end of the day, I would lie awake, reflecting on what had befallen me, my city, my life.

Khan Younis—a city as lovely as a bride in constant splendor—was slowly becoming rubble. Every day I watched residential buildings crushed like shells folding into themselves, towers reduced to mountains of debris, streets emptied of breath. Between one tent and another were stories unfinished. Lives inching toward their end. Memories forged by pain.

One night, precisely at 7:00 p.m., missiles began raining down from sea, land, and sky. We didn't know where they were landing, or what was happening outside our tent. Contacting relatives in other displacement areas wasn't easy. Most of the time, we relied on broadcast news channels, but that too was difficult, because electricity had been cut off almost entirely from the first hours of the aggression.

We lingered in shock, unsure what to do, hoping for clarity as fires blazed where missiles hit nearby. The air filled with the stench of white phosphorus, suffocating us.

The Israeli occupation army invaded our area without evacuation warnings. Tanks and bulldozers advanced from the hill known as Al-Muharrarat. Their vehicles pushed forward into the farmland that had been our refuge. Tanks fired shells at people cowering in tents. An armored vehicle loaded with soldiers flying a yellow flag* approached the gates of the farm. We heard rockets whistling from every direction. The screech of bullets and shells pierced the air again and again.

Still, despite our fear and dread, my younger cousin and I cooked a meal—canned "luncheon" meat, the sort we scorned

---

*The yellow flag is the emblem of Chabad, an orthodox Jewish movement that opposes the existence of Palestinians in land claimed by Israel.

before the genocide, mixed with bell peppers, onions, and spices. We stirred it over a slow fire, poured it into a broad white dish, and served it with some green olives.

Though humble and simple, the food was delicious. We just wanted to eat together. The tanks had drawn closer, and we knew we could meet our maker at any moment.

The shelling intensified. We decided to have our Nescafé—a habit we refused to give up, even though supplies of it had been cut off when the borders closed. We served it alongside all the kinds of biscuits we'd managed to buy—cravings born in wartime—even though these same biscuits were supposed to be part of the free food aid offered to our hungry people.

By 9:00 p.m., the roar of the Israeli tanks had grown louder. Still, we laughed and joked together. Some of our relatives were shocked that we were so set on preparing supper and had such an appetite for coffee and cookies while the Israeli military was rolling toward us. What surprised them most was our absurd laughter—we, who'd been forced from our home, narrowly escaping being buried alive under the rubble, to a place we believed would be safe.

We heard someone yell, "Help! Help!"

It was our neighbor Abu Bassam, from next to the farm. A tank shell had penetrated the wall where he sat, shrapnel striking him and his children. But we couldn't help, and soon his cries stopped. We don't know what became of him and his family. Had any of the neighbors managed to save them?

From our vantage, Israeli fire rained all around. It was nearly impossible to leave. The Israeli armored vehicle with the yellow flag was right at the gate, promising more killing. The firing didn't stop. It wrapped our night in blood. None of us expected to survive.

At first light, we peered through the holes the shells had blown in the gate. No tanks. No bulldozers. My uncle ventured out to see who was left in the area. He found an old man in a white galabia, his bearded face pale, cowering in fear that a sniper or hovering quadcopter might pick him off. He had returned to retrieve some of his things and warned us that an Israeli tank was dug in on the hill, watching. The other tanks were advancing toward the Al-Khair Hospital in Al-Mawasi. He urged us to evacuate immediately.

His words sent panic through us. At first, we were too afraid to move, terrified of the drone above shooting anything that moved. But we had to go.

We gathered our belongings and went out in groups—so that if the first group was struck, the second might survive to collect our remains. That's what we thought.

I left with my sisters and female cousins, walking cautiously through the alleyways. After enough time had passed to ensure that we had survived, the second group followed.

The tents and homes nearby had been burned to the ground. I saw craters from the shells that had hit Abu Bassam's house and later inquired about him. "He and his children were taken to the Abu Yusuf al-Najjar Hospital in Rafah," they said.

People stared at us, wide-eyed in astonishment, when we made it out. They couldn't believe we had survived after everything that had happened to us the night before.

We crossed more than 5 kilometers on foot, walking on a road packed with others fleeing Khan Younis to Rafah, hoping it might be safer.

In the crush of the large crowds, my sister and I became separated from the rest of our family. We decided to continue on to the Shakoush neighborhood in Mawasi, Rafah—a place my uncle had mentioned—hoping we'd reunite there. She and I stopped to rest after hours of walking and glancing over our shoulders. We sat with other displaced people, watching the road and trying to reach our siblings or any member of the family. To no avail.

Finally, after nightfall, we made contact and found each other. Together, we built a new tent and slept close to one another. If death came, we would go together. And if life allowed, we would go on together.

Acknowledgments

This collection of young voices in Gaza during the genocide that began on October 8, 2023, was a labor of love for everyone involved. There was an early iteration that was going to be published by Palestine Writes Press, the publishing arm of the Palestine Writes Literature Festival. We wish to thank the following people for their effort in that version: Susan Muaddi Darraj, Eman Ghanayem, Ibrahim AlAzza, and Zahi Khamis. A special thanks to Hamada elKept, an artist from Gaza whose stunning work features on the cover of this book.

We switched gears when Simon and Schuster made us an offer. Huzama Habayeb did a thorough editing in Arabic, and the English translation was redone.

We are grateful to Rola Harb and Alessandra Bastagli at One Signal for taking on and managing the publication of this anthology; to everyone at Simon & Schuster who helped bring this book to life and deliver it for readers; and to Anjali Singh, of the Anjali Singh Agency, for shopping it around in the first place.

These voices have been unfiltered and uncensored. During the months of Israeli's brutal assault on Gaza, many people rightly criticized the western media for repeating falsehoods, refusing to speak directly about the genocide, failing to ask politicians hard questions, and essentially working to disappear Palestinian perspectives.

Palestine Writes Press was founded as the publishing arm of the Palestine Writes Literature Festival, an institution for

Palestinian cultural workers around the world; and the Culture and Free Thought Association works to nurture the Palestinian body, spirit, and potential in any way possible. In the spirit of these organizations, we are honored to collect these important voices of Palestinians who lived, and continue to live, through a holocaust.

Atria Books, an imprint of Simon & Schuster, fosters an open environment where ideas flourish, bestselling authors soar to new heights, and tomorrow's finest voices are discovered and nurtured. Since its launch in 2002, Atria has published hundreds of bestsellers and extraordinary books, which would not have been possible without the invaluable support and expertise of its team and publishing partners. Thank you to the Atria Books colleagues who collaborated on *Every Moment is a Life,* as well as to the hundreds of professionals in the Simon & Schuster advertising, audio, communications, design, ebook, finance, human resources, legal, marketing, operations, production, sales, supply chain, subsidiary rights, and warehouse departments who help Atria bring great books to light.

Editorial
Rola Harb

Jacket Design
James Iacobelli
Kelli McAdams

Marketing
Annie Probert

Managing Editorial
Paige Lytle
Shelby Pumphrey
Sofia Echeverry
Abby Borchers

Production
Emma Navarro
Lisa Erwin
Patricia Fogarty
Kyoko Watanabe
Imad Harb

Publicity
Shida Carr
Molly Burgoyne

Publishing Office
Dana Trocker
Abby Velasco

Subsidiary Rights
Nicole Bond
Sara Bowne
Rebecca Justiniano

About the Contributors

Abdallah Al-Sayyed is a community activist who works at the Culture and Free Thought Association.

عبد الله السيد، ناشط مجتمعي، يعمل في جمعية الثقافة والفكر الحر.

Ali Abu-Zayed, a graduate of the Bachelor of Arabic Language and Media from Al-Azhar University, writes content, is a community and media activist, and is interested in environmental issues and human sciences.

علي أبو زايد، حاصل على درجة البكالوريوس في اللغة العربية والإعلام من جامعة الأزهر، كاتب محتوى، وناشط مجتمعي وإعلامي، لديه اهتمام بالقضايا البيئية والعلوم الإنسانية.

Amrou Al-Najar is 27 years old. He's an interior designer, musician, singer, stage and film actor.

عمرو النجار، 27 عاماً، مصمم ديكور وموسيقي ومطرب وممثل مسرحي وسينمائي.

Diana Islayh is a university student studying literature, social science, and English. She is interested in music and literature, especially poetry, as well as all things to do with spirituality.

ديانا صليح، طالبة جامعية تدرس الأدب والعلوم الاجتماعية واللغة الإنجليزية. لديها اهتمام بالموسيقى والأدب، خصوصاً الشعر، وبكل ما يتعلق بعالم الروحانيات.

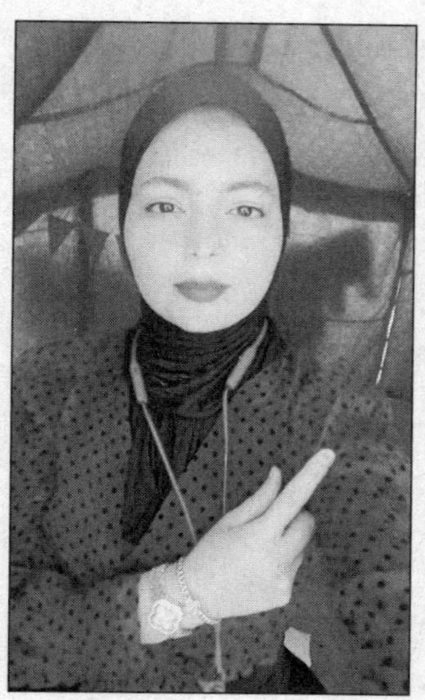

Fatma Asfour holds a BA in English literature. She is a community activist and fashion designer.

فاطمة عصفور، حاصلة على درجة البكالوريوس في الأدب الإنجليزي، وهي ناشطة مجتمعية ومصممة أزياء.

Ghassan Salam holds a Bachelor's degree in Social Work with a concentration in Social and Family Development from Al-Quds University in Palestine. He has completed several professional trainings, including creative writing, elderly care, psychological counseling, women's and human rights.

غسان سلام، حاصل على درجة البكالوريوس في الخدمة الاجتماعية، تخصص التنمية الاجتماعية والأسرية من جامعة القدس في فلسطين. وقد أتمّ عدة دورات تدريبية تشمل الكتابة الإبداعية، والتعامل مع المسنين، والإرشاد النفسي، وحقوق المرأة وحقوق الإنسان.

Khadija Abu-Lebdeh specializes in office management and automation. She works in the fields of writing and broadcasting.

خديجة أبو لبدة، متخصصة في إدارة المكاتب والأتمتة، وتعمل في مجالي الكتابة والإذاعة.

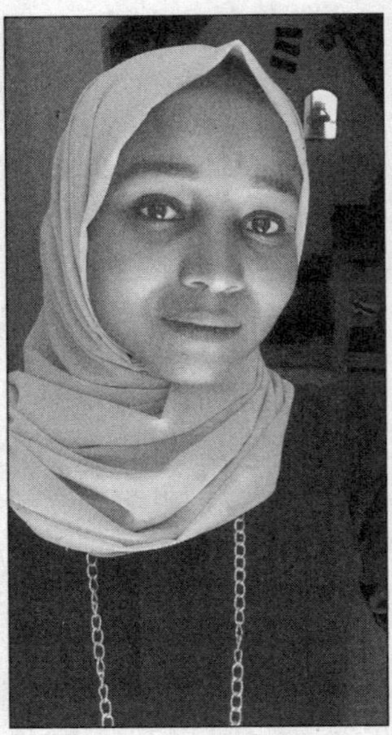

Khuloud Abu-Zaher is a youth activist, a graduate in Arabic language and media from Al-Azhar University. Her hobbies are sewing and fashion design, and she is passionate about community work.

خلود أبو ظاهر، ناشطة شبابية، حاصلة على درجة البكالوريوس في اللغة العربية والإعلام من جامعة الأزهر. من هواياتها الخياطة وتصميم الأزياء، وهي شغوفة بالعمل المجتمعي.

Lubna Meqdad holds a degree in Arabic language from Al-Aqsa University. She worked as a high school teacher for an educational initiative during the genocide. She is an advocate and activist for children, and leads creative writing training for young women.

لبنى مقداد، حاصلة على درجة البكالوريوس في اللغة العربية من جامعة الأقصى. عملت معلِّمة لطلبة الثانوية العامة ضمن مبادرة تعليمية أثناء الإبادة الجماعية. وهي ناشطة تقوم بالعديد من المبادرات للأطفال، ومدرِّبة للكتابة الابداعية لليافعات.

Maram Hammou is a general surgery medical student. She wants to use science as a tool to serve humanity, to create a bridge of knowledge toward a better life for communities in need.

مرام حمو، طالبة طب بشري وجراحة عامة، تسعى إلى استخدام العلم كأداة لخدمة الإنسانيّة، وبناء جسر من المعرفة نحو حياة أفضل للمجتمعات المحتاجة.

Muhammad Mu'ammar is a Palestinian artist and writer. He works as an English teacher and a trainer in the arts of folk dabke, singing, composing, and playing musical instruments, particularly oudautomation. He works in the fields of writing and broadcasting.

محمد معمر، فنان وكاتب فلسطيني، يعمل معلّماً للغة الانجليزية ومدرباً في فنون الدبكة الشعبية والمسرح والغناء والتلحين والعزف على الآلات الموسيقية، ولا سيّما العود. كما يعمل في مجالي الكتابة والإذاعة.

Maysa Salama, from Khan Yunis, holds a Master's degree in Sustainable Development from Al-Quds University. She believes that knowledge is a responsibility and that writing is an act of survival.

ميساء سلامة، من مدينة خان يونس، حاصلة على الماجستير في التنمية المستدامة وبناء المؤسسات من جامعة القدس. "أؤمن أن المعرفة مسؤولية، وأن الكتابة فعل بقاء".

Nebal Najjar, 28 years old, was born and lived all her life in Khuza'a, a village in the Khan Younis district. She is a survivor of four wars, now surviving the fifth, an evolving genocide. She obtained a Bachelor's degree in Applied Chemistry in 2015, and was a student of pharmacy before the genocide started. Between multiple displacements over the past two years, she began writing stories as an escape from the darkness and rubble around her.

نبال النجار، 28 عاماً، وُلدت وعاشت طوال حياتها في قرية خزاعة في محافظة خان يونس. نجت من أربع حروب، وتعيش اليوم فصول إبادة جماعية تتكشف تباعاً. حصلت على درجة البكالوريوس في الكيمياء التطبيقية عام 2015، وكانت تدرس الصيدلة قبل اندلاع هذه الإبادة. وبين موجات النزوح المتكررة خلال العامين الماضيين، بدأت تكتب القصص، كفسحة ضوء تنتشلها من الظلام والركام من حولها.

Rizq Ahmad graduated with a degree in business administration. He works as a community initiatives coordinator. During the genocide, he worked on educational initiatives and on creating safe spaces for women in the absence of health and social services.

رزق أحمد، حاصل على شهادة في إدارة الأعمال، ويعمل منسقاً للمبادرات المجتمعية. خلال الإبادة الجماعية، شارك في مبادرات تعليمية، وفي إنشاء مساحات آمنة للنساء في ظل غياب الخدمات الصحية والاجتماعية.

Reema Abu-Mousa is a pharmacist and is active in community health education.

ريما أبو موسى، صيدلانية، وناشطة في مجال التوعية الصحية والمجتمعية.

Samya Al-Laham is a high school student and activist, and writes from the city of Khan Younis.

سامية اللحام، طالبة في المرحلة الثانوية، وناشطة، تكتب من مدينة خان يونس.

Saja Laham is 23 years old. She specializes in basic and early-childhood education. During the genocide, she worked as a volunteer teacher.

سجا اللحام، 23 عاماً، متخصصة في التعليم الأساسي ومرحلة الطفولة المبكرة. خلال الإبادة الجماعية، عملت معلّمة متطوعة لتدريس الأطفال.

Samah Abu-Awwad graduated with a degree in psychology and counseling from Al-Aqsa University. She worked as a psychological counselor and children's activist during the genocide.

سماح أبو عواد، حاصلة على درجة البكالوريوس في علم النفس والإرشاد من جامعة الأقصى. عملت أثناء الإبادة الجماعية مرشدة نفسية للأطفال.

ONE SIGNAL
PUBLISHERS
ATRIA

كل دقيقة حياة

غزة في زمن الإبادة الجماعية

جمع وإشراف

سوزان أبو الهوى

تحرير

حزامة حبايب | العربية

سوزان أبو الهوى | الإنجليزية

ترجمة

سوزان أبو الهوى

كاي هيكينن

مشروع تعاون بين

مؤسسة "فلسطين تكتب" وجمعية الثقافة والفكر الحر

ONE SIGNAL PUBLISHERS

ATRIA

NEW YORK AMSTERDAM/ANTWERP LONDON

TORONTO SYDNEY/MELBOURNE NEW DELHI

فهرس المحتويات

كل دقيقة حياة

مقدمة | بحثاً عن غزة

سوزان أبو الهوى

كثيرون منّا أدركوا منذ الثامن من أكتوبر 2023 أنّ إسرائيل كانت ستطلق العنان للفانتازيا العسكرية للصهيونية، التي ظلّوا يتحدّثون عنها طوال عقدين على الأقل. ففي العديد من الأوساط السياسية والاقتصادية والأكاديمية والاجتماعية داخل المجتمع الإسرائيلي، كانت قد تعالت منذ زمن بعيد دعواتٌ صريحة إلى "قتلهم جميعاً"، قبل أن تقود سبعة عقود من نضال الفلسطينيين، أبناء الأرض الأصليين، إلى "طوفان الأقصى" في السابع من أكتوبر.

بذلنا جميعاً، نحن في الشتات وأصحاب الضمائر الحيَّة، قصارى جهدنا لإيجاد وسيلة لإيصال المساعدات إلى غزة. كان الأمر ضرباً من المستحيل، لكن بعد محاولات فاشلة، وجدتُ نفسي على الجانب الآخر من المستحيل، في غزة الحبيبة، في فلسطين، وذلك في شهر فبراير 2024.

من خلال منظمة "ملاعب من أجل فلسطين" Playgrounds for Palestine، تمكنّا من إدخال المساعدات الإغاثية، ونفَّذنا مشاريع محلية للأطفال. ثم عدتُ إلى غزة مرة أخرى بعد شهر.

قهوة، و"مداواة روحية"

لن أكرِّر هنا ما سبق أن كتبتُه وتحدثتُ عنه بصورة مفصَّلة سوى أنني كنت شاهدة، في مصر، على ما لا يمكن وصفه إلا بمهزلة المساعدات الإنسانية، عبر استعراض كانت تقوم به منظمة واحدة على الأقل، تتلقى الأموال بلا حسيب ولا رقيب، ثم تُرسل إلى غزة شاحنات محمَّلة بصناديق شبه فارغة.

وحين تمكّنتُ من دخول غزة، بنفسي، في فبراير 2024 ثم في أبريل من العام نفسه، حملتُ ما استطعت من الحقائب: أكثر من عشرين حقيبة في الرحلة الأولى، وأربعين في الثانية.

كانت المساعدات التي جلبناها معنا مجرَّد قطرة في بحر الحاجة آنذاك. لكنها كانت مهمةً للغاية لمن وصلتهم. وقد حظيت القهوة بالترحيب الأكبر بين الطواقم الطبية والأصدقاء، حيث حملتُ معي نحو عشرة كيلوغرامات منها، مما منحني شعبيَّةً على الفور، فقد حُرم معظم أهل غزة من أبسط أشكال الكرامة: أنْ يبدأوا صباحهم بفنجان قهوة.

لقد سُلب منهم كل شيء، كل شيء ما عدا كرامتهم وإيمانهم وإنسانيتهم. كثيراً ما كنتُ أشعر بالخجل أمامهم، وقد غمروني بكرمهم وطيبتهم وحسن ضيافتهم، هم الذين لم يكن لديهم سوى القليل جداً ليقدموه، ومع ذلك أعطوا بسخاء. عندما غادرتُ غزة في المرة الأولى، ثم في المرة الثانية، تلقيتُ ما يكفي من الهدايا لملء حقيبة صغيرة: سلاسل مفاتيح يدوية الصنع، وقبَّعة محبوكة، وسواراً من الخرز، وقطعة قماش مطرزة، ورسومات.

بالطبع حرصتُ، أثناء وجودي هناك على جمع أكبر قدر ممكن من القصص، معظمها من نساء كنَّ يتعافين في المستشفى.

غالباً ما كانت حكاياتهن تتضمن تفاصيل ومعلومات لم يعرفنها إلا بعد وقوع الأحداث، حيث روينها بنوع من الانفصال، إلى أنْ تعمَّقتُ في السؤال والتقصّي: "كيف كان الصوت؟ كيف كانت الرائحة؟ ما هو الشعور الذي انتابك؟ ما أول خاطر تبادر إلى ذهنك؟".

سمحن لي بطرح أسئلتي عليهن، وكُنَّ كريمات في إجاباتهن. عندها، انهمرت الدموع؛ لتحيطهن النساء من حولهن بالمواساة والعطف. أخبرنني جميعاً أنَّ تلك الأمسيات التي قضيناها معاً كانت المرة الأولى التي يسترجعن فيها مثل هذه التفاصيل، بل والأولى التي يروينها.

ما كان يُفترض أن يكون مجرد جلسة لجمع الشهادات تحول إلى شكل من أشكال المداواة الروحية المرتبطة بوجع السكان الأصليين ومعاناتهم؛ عالم النساء الفلسطينيات اللاتي تشاركن أحلك لحظاتهن وأكثرها رعباً في خضم إبادة جماعية

لا تزال مستمرة. هكذا كانت جداتنا يداوين جراحهن ويضمدن آلامهن، في ظل الأمان العاطفي الذي وفرته نساء أخريات احتوين كلماتهن بحنوّ واحتضنّها برفق، ومنحن بعضهن بعضاً من السلوى والمحبة. شعرتُ بأن هذه التجربة غيَّرتني، وما زلتُ أحمل هؤلاء النساء وحكاياتهن معي.

في النهاية، وجدتُ طريقة مختلفة لأقدِّم شيئاً لشعبنا.

ماجدة ومها، وجمعية الثقافة والفكر الحر

على الرغم من أن حركتي كانت مقيَّدة داخل منشأة طبية معظم الوقت خلال رحلتي الأولى، فإنني تمكنتُ من التنقُّل بمفردي عدة مرات. سألتني صديقتاي العزيزتان ماجدة السقا ومها الراعي ما إذا كان بالإمكان أنْ أنظِّم ورشة كتابة لعدد من الشباب والشابات في "جمعية الثقافة والفكر الحر"، فوافقتُ دون تردُّد، وتمكنّا من عقد جلستين قبل أن أضطر إلى مغادرة غزة في المرة الأولى. لكن خلال رحلتي الثانية، بعد أقل من شهر، كنتُ أتمتَّع بحرية أكبر في التنقل، وجعلتُ ورش الكتابة أولوية.

كانت ماجدة وعائلتها قد نزحوا من بيت العائلة التاريخي الكبير في خان يونس، حيث استقبلتهم مها الراعي وعائلتها في بيتهم في رفح. وقد حظيتُ بشرف الإقامة معهم لليلتين، إذ كنّا ننام جميعاً على الأرض في صفوف متجاورة. تقاسموا معي طعامهم، بل وأصرّوا عليَّ ذات مرة بأن أقبل ماء الاستحمام الذي سخّنوه لي على موقد خارجي. كان وجودي بينهم تجربةً مفعمةً بالامتنان، محاطة بالكرم من أناس لم يتبقَّ لديهم سوى القليل. هذا العطاء والانفتاح والمشاركة وروح العائلة التي جمعتنا فوراً شكَّلت تجسيداً للمجتمع الفلسطيني في غزة أثناء إبادة جماعية متكاملة الأركان.

وفي النهاية، قصفت إسرائيل منزل مها، ليتحول ذلك البيت الذي كان يفيض بالحب إلى ركام، واضطر الجميع إلى البحث عن ملجأ في مكان آخر. ولحسن الحظ، نجوا جميعاً من القصف.

فكرة الأنطولوجيا

كان هؤلاء الكتّاب الواعدون جميعهم قد نزحوا من بيوتهم. كلُّ واحد منهم فقد أحبّة له جرّاء العدوان الإسرائيلي المتواصل. جميعهم شهدوا وسمعوا وشعروا بما يفوق التصور. خصَّصنا الساعتين الأوليين في الجلسة لبعض التمارين الكتابية، إذ كنتُ أرغب في التعرُّف على أساليبهم في الكتابة، واستكشاف ما تنطوي عليه نصوصهم من قيمة أدبية، لكن الغاية الأهم من هذه التمارين كانت أن نتعارف ونبني جوّاً من الثقة.

لم أكن قد التقيتُ أياً منهم قبل تلك الورشة الأولى. تراوحت أعمارهم بين أوائل العشرينيات ومنتصف الثلاثينيات. وقد بدا واضحاً من التمارين الكتابية الأولى أن بعضهم يمتلكون موهبة حقيقية، ويمكنهم بالفعل كتابة نصوص سردية ذات مستوى أدبي رفيع. عندها، أدركتُ أن أهم ما يمكنني أن أقدّمه وسط هذه الإبادة الجماعية هو مشاركة ما لديّ من مهارات لتمكين كتّاب صاعدين. فالفلسطينيون في غزة هم أصحاب رواية هذه اللحظة التاريخية. هم أبطالها وهم ضحاياها، وهم الأرض والغرس.

ومن هنا، وُلدت فكرة هذه الأنطولوجيا.

ورش الكتابة

أقيمت ورش الكتابة على الشاطئ وفي فناء "جمعية الثقافة والفكر الحر" (CFTA)، تحت الأزيز المتواصل لـ "الزنّانات"، أي المسيَّرات الإسرائيلية، وأصوات القنابل البعيدة التي لم تهدأ. وكان بعض الكتّاب يستغرقون ساعتين للوصول إلى مكان انعقاد الورش، لا لبعد المسافة، بل بسبب صعوبة التنقل داخل منطقة المواصي المكتظة، في خان يونس، بعد أن هجَّرَ الجيش الإسرائيلي غالبية سكان شمال غزة وحشرهم فيها. وسواء جاؤوا بعربة يجرُّها حمار، أو بسيارة، أو بدراجة هوائية، فإن أقصى سرعة كانوا يستطيعون بلوغها كانت تتراوح بين ثمانية وخمسة وعشرين كيلومتراً في الساعة.

بعد التمارين الكتابية، طلبتُ من كلّ واحد منهم أن يكتب قصة أو قصيدة أو أغنية أو مذكرات، أو أي نص آخر، قصيراً كان أو طويلاً. في لقائنا التالي، تناوبوا

على قراءة نصوصهم، واحداً تلو الآخر، أعقب ذلك تلقّي ملاحظات من زملائهم ومنّي. مضت الجلسات على هذا النحو، حيث كنا نخوض نقاشات حول أساليب الكتابة، والتقنيات الأدبية، وبناء الحبكة، ومختلف عناصر السرد المؤثّر.

كانت بعض المسودات الأولى مكتوبة بأسلوب أقرب إلى تقارير عن حياتهم، فكان التركيز الأكبر في عملنا على جعل القصة "أصغر حجماً"، من خلال توجيه السرد نحو التفاصيل الحسية الدقيقة، التي تنبثق منها القصة الأكبر عن الإبادة الجماعية من دون الحاجة إلى التصريح بها مباشرة. وكانت النتيجة مذهلة. فمع تركيزهم على التفاصيل الدقيقة – كرائحة الخُبز الطازج وهو يُخبز في الصباح، وملمس الغبار على بشرتهم، والصمت المدوي في آذانهم بعد الانفجار، ونغمة صوت أمّ تنادي أبناءها للعودة إلى البيت – أصبحت قصصهم نابضة بالحياة، تكاد تُرى وتُحس. لم تعد السرديات مجرد تسجيل للأحداث بل تجارب غامرة، تستدرج القارئ إلى قلب واقعهم.

كنتُ أراقب ثقتهم بأنفسهم تنمو وتتعزز مع كل جلسة، حيث أصبحت أصواتهم أكثر قوة ووضوحاً وثباتاً. ساد فيما بينهم شعور جليٌّ بالتضامن والاحترام المتبادل. بكى بعضهم أثناء قراءة كلماتهم الخاصة، وفي بعض الأحيان كانوا يسمعون التفاصيل تُروى بصوت عالٍ لأول مرة. بكينا معهم. لم يكن هؤلاء الكتّاب يصقلون مهاراتهم فحسب، بل كانوا أيضاً يجدون القوة الكامنة في قصصهم، بوصفهم أبناء وبنات الأرض الأصليين في زمن الإبادة الاستعمارية.

الكتّاب، الحب

تولى ماهر داود (أبو محمود)، الذي يعمل في جمعية غزة للثقافة والفكر الحر (CFTA)، تنظيم وإدارة كل جلسة، حريصاً على التواصل مع الكتّاب وتأمين وصولهم من وإلى موقع اللقاءات. وقد قرأ القصص واختار الكتّاب النهائيين، وتولّى المراجعة اللغوية لمسودة مبكرة من المخطوطة. وككل كاتب في هذه المختارات، خاطر كثيراً ليتمكن من الحضور، محاولاً أن يقتنص لحظات من الحياة العادية في زمن فقد كل معنى لما هو عادي؛ بلا زوجته وطفله، وبلا كهرباء يمكن الاعتماد عليها لشحن هاتفه، وبلا أي ضمانة للماء والغذاء والمأوى.

كل واحد من هؤلاء الكُتّاب كان يرزح تحت صدمة هائلة، تنطق بها عيونهم وتثقل معها أجسادهم. أحببتُهم جميعاً، وأشعر أنني تغيرتُ بسببهم. كان عمرو النجار عادةً ما يفتتح جلساتنا أو يختتمها بأغنية بصوته الشجي. لقد حولت الإبادة الجماعية حياته المنظمة إلى فوضى، وكان يقضي أيامه في محاولة جمع أجزاء مبعثرة لم تعد تترابط، كأنْ يسعى للحصول على فنجان قهوة في الصباح، وهو ترف صار بعيد المنال في حياته الجديدة.

كانت ديانا صليح تميل إلى الصمت في العادة، حتى عندما كانت تقرأ، بالكاد يُسمع صوتها تحت الأزيز المروّع للمسيَّرات الإسرائيلية. قالت لي شيئاً عابراً ظلَّ عالقاً في ذهني: "حياتي لا تشبهني"، ثم أضافت: "المخيف أنني تكيفتُ معها . . . كأنني أصبحتُ شخصاً آخر". كانت النسخة الأولى من قصة ديانا مكتملة الملامح، وحرَّكت مشاعرنا جميعاً.

بالمثل، كانت مرام حمو ذات صوت هادئ، وكان الحزن على فقدان عمَّتها يخنق صوتها مع كل قراءة. كانت طالبة في السنة الثالثة في كلية الطب، وقد رأت جامعتها تختفي بين عشية وضحاها، وهو ما تركها في حالة ذهول وضياع. بدت وكأنها تتشبَّث بأي خيط أمل، بأي شيء يشبه التشجيع الذي اعتادت أن تتلقّاه من عمَّتها الحبيبة.

ظلت ريما أبو موسى متحفِّظة. كانت تعتمل لديها مشاعر الغضب والإحباط أكثر من الذهول. وحين كانت تقرأ نصها أمام المجموعة، كان الجميع يومئون تفهمّاً. ورغم أنني أستطيع أن أتخيَّل حجم الألم الذي يحفر عميقاً في حياتهم، أدرك بأنني لا أستطيع أبداً أن أفهمه تماماً. لكنني بالتأكيد أجد في الغضب نعمة يمكنني التماهي معها. من ناحيتهما، شرعت سامية اللحام وابنة عمها سجا اللحام في هذه الرحلة الكتابية معاً. جرَّبت كلٌّ منهما كتابة عدة قصص، جميعها كانت مؤثرة. كان من الممتع مشاهدتهما وهما تغربلان العديد من الأحداث الكبرى، قبل أن تستقرا أخيراً على لحظات فردية. بالنسبة لسامية، كان لقاءً عابراً لكنه عميق مع رجل مسنّ أصلح لها حذاءها. أما سجا، فقد خطّت على الورق اللحظة التي انقلبت فيها حياتها من البيت إلى النزوح. كنتُ أراهما تتبادلان الحديث من خلال النظرات، في تواصل دافئ ورقيق بين روحين، تشدُّ إحداهما على يد الأخرى.

كانت فاطمة عصفور دوماً الأكثر أناقةً بيننا جميعاً. حتى في ظل الحرمان في تلك الأشهر العصيبة، كانت تولي اهتماماً خاصاً بأناقتها. كانت ملابسها وشعرها

وأحذيتها مرتبة ومنسقة، بقدر ما سمحت به الظروف. كانت تمشي كعارضة أزياء، رأسها مرفوع وكتفاها مشدودتان. خاضت رحلة خطيرة على دراجة هوائية، مجازفة بكل شيء لإنقاذ ملابسها، ولم تعتذر عمّا فعلت. خلافاً للآخرين، لم تكن خلود أبو ظاهر تظهر ألمها. كان الألم حاضراً بلا شك، لكنه تواري خلف إصرار جريء وواثق على العمل والإنتاج. كانت تأتي مستعدة، وتقوم بكل الواجبات المسندة إليها، ولم يكن لديها وقت لإضاعته في الحزن، على الأقل ليس في ورش الكتابة. كانت تصغي بانتباه إلى ملاحظات الآخرين النقدية، وتبدي رأيها في نصوصهم بصراحة ووضوح. لقد كان حضورها حقيقياً ومؤثراً.

أما رزق أحمد فكان روحاً وديعة، يحمل إحساساً عميقاً بالعائلة. بدا جليّاً من كتاباته وطريقة حديثه أنه محصّن بروابط عائلية قوية وحميمة. ومع أن هذا أمر مألوف في العائلات الفلسطينية، إلا أن هذا الدفء كان لافتاً في حالته على نحو خاص. كان قادراً على الصمود، بل وإيجاد الفرح والبهجة حتى وهو يعيش في خيمة معتمداً على مساعدات ضئيلة، بعد حياة ميسورة، طالما أنهم معاً. وهذا بالضبط ما يرويه نصُّه.

من ناحيتها، كانت لبنى مقداد تبحث عن خاتمة سعيدة، عن بارقة أمل وسط ما لا يُحتمل. كانت تجربتها في تفادي القنابل، بالمعنى الحرفي، وتنقُّلها من خيمة إلى أخرى والعيش على طعام لم يكونوا ليستهلكوه أبداً في الأوقات العادية مروّعةً (وإن لم تكن استثناءً بين الفلسطينيين في غزة). لكنها كانت تُنهي كل ما تقوله تقريباً بمشاعر مفعمة بالأمل، كعلامة ترقيم لا تقوى على تحمُّل أو تصديق الجملة التي تسبقها. كانت ابتسامتها الحذرة، لكن الواثقة، تجسّد البحث عن الضوء المنشود في العتمة. ميساء سلامة كانت كذلك أيضاً، مصرَّة على أن تنتهي القصص في الحياة وعلى الورق بانتصار المقاومة الذي يحيِّر جميع المستعمرين على مر العصور. إنه ذاك الإصرار الفريد المتجذِّر في أبناء الأرض الأصليين لانتزاع الحياة من بين أنياب الموت، هذا الإصرار النابع من الارتباط الأبدي بالأرض والقبيلة.

بدت خديجة أبو لبدة منذ البداية وكأنها ستكتب عن شقيقها الحبيب. وكانت الطريقة التي اختارت بها أن تستحضره وتخلّد ذكراه في نصها الأدبي مدهشة ومؤثرة. في حين أنَّ قصة محمد أبو معمر تُذكّرنا جميعاً بأن الأشياء التي نحلم بها ونتمناها ليست دائماً ما نحتاج إليه. هو وخديجة كانا قاصَّيْن بالفطرة.

كان عبدالله السيد يحمل ابتسامة عريضة لم تكن تفارقه، تُخفي خلفها وجع أب وزوج يكابد لتأمين أبسط مقومات الحياة لأسرته. ولم يكن علي أبو زايد يختلف

عنه. على الرغم من اختلاف شخصيتيهما في الطباع وأسلوب الكتابة والطاقة التي يشيعها حضورهما، فإن كلاً منهما كان يذكرني بالآخر. كانا طيبين، ومراعيين، وكريمين، على قدر من النزاهة والمروءة، ما يجعل العالم أكثر اتزاناً. كانا يناضلان لتوفير احتياجات عائلتيهما الصغيرتين، ومع ذلك لم يتخلَّفا عن حضور ورش الكتابة، حريصين على المشاركة في أي جهد ثقافي وفكري مهما بلغت الظروف من قسوة. أما سماح أبو عواد، فهي شاعرة في جوهرها. لقد أذهلتني غنائية نثرها، أكثر حتى من مساهمتها الرائعة نفسها.

بالإضافة إلى إتاحة المجال للحواس، كان أحد الأمور التي ركّزنا عليها في ورش الكتابة هو الصدق العاطفي والاجتماعي والسياسي. كنتُ أشجعهم على الغوص عميقاً، وعدم ممارسة الرقابة الذاتية عند مقاربة ما يُعتبر من "المحرَّمات". وقد وعت نبال النجار هذا الدرس، فشقَّت طريقها عكس التيار السائد وسط أهلها ووطنها، عازمةً على الرحيل دون أن تلقي نظرةً إلى الوراء. من الطبيعي أن يشعر المرء بمثل هذه الأشياء، دون أن يعني ذلك أنه لا يشعر بنقيضها تماماً في أوقات أخرى، أو حتى في الوقت نفسه. كنتُ فخورة بها لجرأتها في كتابة ما قد لا يرغب بقية العالم في سماعه من الفلسطينيين.

على نحو مماثل، بدأ علي أبو زايد بكتابة قصة جميلة ثانية عن سعيه لتأمين خيمة صغيرة، تمنحه وزوجته لحظةً من الخصوصية والحميمية. كنتُ أتمنى لو استطعنا أن نضم تلك القصة هنا، لكن مشاغل الحياة والمسؤوليات لم تترك لعلي الوقت الكافي لإتمامها.

من القصص التي أثَّرت فيّ بعمق قصة لشاب يدعى غسان سلام. كان طويلاً ووسيماً، يشعُّ بهالة من اللطف والطيبة. لم يحضر غسان سوى ورشتين، لكن المسودة الأولى لقصته ظلت عالقة في ذهني. بكاء الطفل في قصته، الذي كان يسمعه دون أن يتمكن من الوصول إليه – في مكان ما في العراء أو تحت الركام حيث كان قناصة الجيش الإسرائيلي يتربَّصون – لا يزال يرنُّ في أذني كلما تذكّرته. وكذلك حواره الداخلي الموجع بصراحته، والعاري من كل تصنُّع، حين قال: "أنا لا شيء". كان كاتباً بالفطرة؛ لذا واصلتُ الإلحاح عليه لكتابة القصة. كان قد فقد هاتفه الذي حفظ فيه النصَّ الأول، لكنه لبّى طلبي في النهاية، وكتب نصّاً آخر. وأنا في غاية الامتنان لأنه فعل ذلك، فنصُّه المؤثِّر من أحبّ القصص إلى قلبي.

حزامة حبايب

بما أنّ المساهمات القصصية مكتوبة في الأصل باللغة العربية، فإنَّ قدرتي على المتابعة وتقديم الإرشادات الكتابية محدودة. صحيح أنني أقرأ وأكتب بلغتي الأم، لكنني لستُ متمكِّنة كفاية لتوجيه الكتّاب لغوياً وأسلوبياً. وهنا تدخّلت صديقتي العزيزة، الروائية اللامعة حزامة حبايب.

اتصلتُ بها بعد أن كنتُ قد أنجزتُ ترجمة المجموعة كاملة، بل وبعد أن قدّمت لنا دار سايمون أند شوستر عقد النشر، فكلُّ نص أدبي يحتاج إلى تحرير وصقل وتشذيب وتطوير، وهو ما لم أكن أستطيع أن أقدمه لهم، على الأقل ليس باللغة العربية. أما هي، فتمتلك القدرة على ذلك، وهو ما قامت به.

وضعت حزامة جانباً ارتباطاتها ومشاريعها الأدبية والتزاماتها الأسرية، وأمضت الشهور الثلاثة التالية تعمل مع كل كاتب وكاتبة. كانت تجربةً فريدة من نوعها بالنسبة لها، وقد سجّلتها في هذه الأنطولوجيا في كلمة المحرِّرة.

كما استعانت أيضاً بالمترجمة كاي هيكنين التي لم تبخل بدورها بوقتها الثمين وسط جدول مزدحم، للمساعدة في الترجمة.

قصص خام وحقيقية

أشعر بالفخر والإعجاب تجاه كل واحد من الكتّاب الذين حضروا ورش الكتابة، وعملوا في ظروف مستحيلة، بلا موارد، أثناء الكتابة وإعادة الكتابة، حيث كانوا يأتون رغم الظروف القاسية، ليختبروا لحظات من التبادل الفكري والإبداعي في وقت كان فيه تأمين الماء والطعام يستنزف معظم أيامهم. كان تطور كتاباتهم في وقت قصير أمراً لافتاً. أحبُّ كل قصة هنا، فهي قصص خام وحقيقية، عاطفية ومدمرة. كل قصة تمثِّل لحظةً إنسانية بسيطة وعادية، تجري في خضم المحرقة التي نعيشها اليوم – شراء الخبز، والذهاب إلى المرحاض، وإصلاح حذاء، ومشاركة وجبة، والعثور على وسيلة تنقُّل، كل ذلك في خلفية أول إبادة جماعية تُبثُّ على الهواء مباشرة، تُعرض على مرأى ومسمع العالم بكل ما فيها من رعب ودموية ومعاناة تفوق الوصف.

بينما جاؤوا ظاهرياً ليتعلَّموا مني، كنتُ أنا من يتعلَّم منهم. لا أعرف كيف يمكن للمرء أن يدفن عائلته دون أن يجد فسحةً للحزن، أن يرى كل مبنى كان يحتضن ذكرياته يتحول إلى ركام، أن يتحمَّل الذل والمهانة إذ يجد نفسه مضطراً لمشاركة المرحاض مع مئات الأشخاص، أن يتدافع مع الحشود من أجل حفنة من الأرز، أن يرتجف من البرد شتاءً ويختنق من الحرّ صيفاً داخل خيمة لا توفر أي حماية، أن يكون عاجزاً عن إعالة أو حماية من يحب، أن يرى الموت ويسمع صرخاته يوماً بعد يوم.

لكنهم يعرفون، وقد أظهروا لي كيف يلملمُ الإنسان نفسه، ليبحث عن الإبداع والجمال.

أُكنُّ لهم جميعاً الإعجاب والاحترام. وكان شرفاً عظيماً لي أن أنقل كل ما أملك من مهارات لهؤلاء الملهمين، من أبناء وبنات فلسطين، ليكونوا هم من يروون هذه اللحظة الفارقة في التاريخ، لأن أصواتهم هي الأجدر بأن تُسمع. لا أعرف كيف أعبِّر عن امتناني أو محبَّتي لهم بما يكفي إلا بأن أجمعهم في هذا الكتاب، ليحبَّهم العالم كما أحببتهم.

رسالة من المحرِّرة | بين تحرير وتحرير: معنى آخر للحب

حزامة حبايب

أن تكتبَ قصصاً في قلب إبادة جارية، يعني أن تشتقَّ حبرَك من قلبك.

أن تقرأ قصصاً عن إبادة في قلب إبادة جارية بلا توقف، يعني أنَّ قلبَك، على أقل تقدير، سيُسحَق.

كمحرِّرة أدبيَّة لهذا المشروع القصصي، لا أعتقد أنني كنتُ مستعدةً للتعامل مع هذا القدر من الرعب والدمار والموت المترصِّد في كل بقعة في غزة، ضمن مناخٍ سرديٍّ لاهث يسحبُك إليه عنوة، فتشعر بأنفاسك تضيق، والمساحة من حولك –أينما كنت– تنكمش، حتى تجد نفسَك محشوراً في خيمة تقبضُ فيها على حياة شحيحة، منتَهَكة، وسط وجوهٍ ذابت ملامحُها. وفي لحظاتٍ من السرد القاسي، يتسارع نبضُك، تحت القصف الإسرائيلي الهمجي، الذي يهزُّ السماوات والأرض، فتجمعُ إليك لحمَك، خشية أن يتمزَّق، قبل أن تكتشفَ أنَّ روحاً تشبه روحَك قد تحولت إلى أشلاء.

• • •

منذ مايو/ أيار 2025، وعلى مدى أكثر من ثلاثة شهور، خضتُ تجربةً استثنائية، في ما قد تكون أول عملية تحرير أدبي تُجْرى بالكامل عبر الواتساب، من خلال النقاش والمتابعة يومياً مع ثمانية عشر كاتباً وكاتبةً في غزة.

كنتُ أتواصل معهم، عن بعد، بين عمّان ودبي. وتعيَّن عليَّ أن أكون يقظةً، مُتنبِّهةً لأي رسالة تضيء موبايلي في آخر الليل أو مع أول ضوء يشقُّ النهار، مدركةً صعوبة تواصل الكتّاب عبر موبايلاتهم في أيِّ وقت، منتظرين وصولَ شبكة الإنترنت إلى أجهزتهم، أو مضطرين إلى قطع طرقاتٍ غير آمنة، في مساحة كلِّها غير آمنة، للوصول إلى نقطة شحن للموبايل.

لم تكن هذه تجربةً تحريريةً أدبيةً بالمعنى التقني، اللغوي والبنائي، فحسب؛ بل كانت تجربةً عاطفيةً. أصعبُ ما فيها حين كنتُ أرسل للكتّاب رسائل "واتساب" متتابعة، فيها إرشادات أو توجيهات، أو اقتراحات بإعادة صياغة، أو استفسار عن دلالةٍ ما أو شخصية بعينها في القصة. كنتُ أنتظر ساعات، وأحياناً أياماً، قبل أن يتحول مؤشّر حالة الرسالة من علامة رمادية واحدة، إلى علامتين رماديتين، ثم زرقاوين.

وفي المسافة بين الرمادي والأزرق، كان قلبي خلالها يظلُّ يخفق، قبل أن يتحول الأمر عندي إلى هوس، حدّ الالتصاق بشاشة موبايلي، أستعجلُها كي تضيء. وكثيراً ما كان الهاجس الأكثر رعباً يطلُّ في رأسي: ماذا لو . . . ؟! لكنني لم أكن أريد أن أصدِّق.

لقد كانت تجربةً مؤلمةً، ومحطِّمةً بطريقتها. ماذا تفعل حين تطلبُ من أحدهم أو إحداهن الردَّ على استفسار في أسرع وقت ممكن؟ ليأتيك الجواب متأخراً: "دفنتُ زوجتي يوم أمس، أرجو أن تتحملّوني فقط إلى حين انتهاء فترة العزاء"، أو "خجلان منكِ.. اليوم تركنا كل ما نملك ونزحنا هاربين للبحر.. للآن ما جهزنا مكاناً نبيت فيه ليلتنا.. أمهليني فقط ثلاثة أيام.. أرجو رحابة صدركم"، أو "إذا في إمكانية، يوم السبت أو الأحد سأقوم بإرسال النسخة النهائية من القصة.. أخي استشهد".

كم كنتُ أشعر بالضآلة، والعجز المطلق!

أنا سيدةُ الكلمات، كما أحبُّ أن أصف نفسي، تخذلني كلماتي، إذ يُختزَل قاموس المواساة لدي بعبارات من نوع: "قلبي معك"، أو "كن قوياً"، أو "حافظي على نفسك". وأحياناً، يبدو كأنني أصدر أمراً مباشراً: "ابقَ حيّاً!".

ثم أخجلُ من نفسي لأنني حيَّة.

"لماذا يجب أن أعيش أنا؟"، فيما على بُعد بضع ساعات مني صبية فلسطينية جميلة، في الثانية والعشرين من العمر، كاتبة واعدة، وطالبة في كلية الطب، لم يتبقَّ لها كلية ترتادها أو جامعة، عاشت سبعة اجتياحات إسرائيلية مدمِّرة لغزة على امتداد عمرها الفتي، بما في ذلك الإبادة الحالية التي نزحت خلالها مع عائلتها ثلاث عشرة مرة، حتى اللحظة. ترتزق من أي عمل متاح لتؤمِّن كيس طحين أو عدس لأسرتها المؤلفة من تسعة أفراد، وقد نهش الجوع أجسادهم. وحين أسألها

عن حالها، ترسل لي رسالةً صوتية عبر الواتساب توثِّقُ صوتَ القذائف والرصاصات المنهمرة من الدبابات وطائرات الكواد كابتر الإسرائيلية، أثناء سيرها في طريقها إلى المستشفى الذي تتدرَّب فيه.

ومع ذلك، كانت هذه التجربة محرِّرةً بطريقتها.

إن "تحرير" في اللغة العربية كلمة مدهشة، فهي تنطوي على معنيين مُلهمَيْن بالقدر نفسه، الأول بمعنى الحرية والتحرُّر، أي الانعتاق أو الإعتاق، أو إطلاق سراح، أو فكّ القيْد بالمعنى المادي والمعنوي؛ والثاني بمعنى تحرير النصوص الكتابية بمختلف أنواعها، في مقدمتها "التحرير الأدبي"، الذي يشمل تحرير النص من الأخطاء اللغوية والنحوية والتركيبية، وتخليصه من الشوائب، وتحسين صياغته، وتطويره. لكن المعنيين يلتقيان، فتحرير النص شكلٌ من أشكال تحريره من القيود، التي تحول دون وصول الفكرة والمعنى، كي يحلِّق في فضاءات تعبيرية أوسع.

وإذا كان من شيء أدين به لهذه الرحلة العاطفية، بدرب الآلام الذي قطعتُه مع هؤلاء المبدعات والمبدعين، فهو أن شجاعتهم، وشغفهم، وحرصهم على إيصال أصواتهم وحكاياتهم، في خضمّ الجحيم الذي يعيشونه، بأي ثمن، حرَّرتني.

وحين أستيقظُ على رسالة من إحداهن، تُهديني أغنيةً بصوتها الدافق بالدفء والعذوبة، أو رسالة من أخرى، تُطمئنني على وضعها، قائلة: "لا تقلقي! أنا أحيا بالأمل"، أعرف أنني اليوم "حرّة"، أكثر من أي وقت مضى.

سوف يَحيون، وسوف يحلمون، وسوف يعشقون، وسوف يكتبون.

هذا زمانهم، فلسطينيون أحرار، خُلقوا للحياة والحب.

قهوة بقرب الأزرق العجوز

محمد معمّر

تفاصيل، تفاصيل كثيرة.

لا أعرف من أين أبدأ، أو ماذا أكتب.

دائماً ما كنتُ أسترسلُ في أي شيء أكتبُه بمجرَّد البدء مباشرة.

لكنني اليوم عاجزٌ حتى عن وصف ما أمرُّ به أو أشعر به.

هذه الفظاعات أنهكتنا، أرهقتنا، مزَّقتنا، وذبحتنا من الوريد إلى الوريد.

استيقظتُ، عيناي نصف مفتوحتين، ورأسي تحت الوسادة، بعد ليلة أخرى من الكوابيس. ليس الأمر بجديد. أصبحت الكوابيس رفيقتي الدائمة في كل ليلة منذ أن بدأت السماء تمطرُ قنابل، وكم لي فيها من صولات وجولات ومعارك شرسة.

كلُّ الحروب تكون بين كرٍّ وفرّ، إلا حربي أنا بين كرٍّ وكرّ، ودائماً أنا الذي أنهيها وأصحو.

بعد نصف ساعة من القتال مع ضوء الشمس والفراش وماء الصنبور والصابون أفقت.

كلمة "صنبور" هنا كناية عن دلوٍ صغير أغرفُ منه الماء لأرشَّ به وجهي. لستُ في بيتي كي أمارسَ الحدَّ الأدنى من الرفاهية، أو حتى أبسط مقومات الحياة.

أنا نازح.

يا لها من تسمية مُلطّفة للمهانة البشرية المطلقة.

أعيش في خيمة صغيرة مثلَّثة الشكل، بنيتُها باستخدام ثلاث خشبات فقط وقطعة من القماش.

بصراحة هي ليست خيمة بمعنى خيمة، لكنها شيء من هذا القبيل.

صحيح أنني لا أستطيع الوقوف داخلها، وصحيح أنني لو مددتُ جسدي في نومي كاملاً سأضربها بقدمي، لكنها على الأقل تسترني وأهلي من البرد والنار. وفسِّر النار هنا بما شِئت.

وعلى ذكر النار، من البديهي أن أقوم بعد استيقاظي بإشعال النار التي أصبحت طقساً صباحياً أبدياً لا بَرَكة في يومك من دونه. زمن الوقود والغاز انتهى. الحياة البدائية هي السائدة هنا، حتى إنني مع هيمنتها المطلقة لم أعد أفكر "كيف سيكون المستقبل؟"، بل بـ"وماذا بعد؟".

"متى سيبدأ العصر الحجري؟"

"وهل سنعود إلى عصور سبقته؟"

أفكار الصباح أمام النار غريبة، ألا تُوافقني الرأي؟

حسناً دعك من خزعبلاتي، وتعال اشرب معي قهوتي التي أصنعها كلما أشعلتُ النار، القهوة التي صرنا نبتاعها بالجرام بعد أن كنا نشتريها بالكيلوغرام.

حاولتُ أن أمتنع عن شربها حقاً، لكنني لم أستطع.

هي جزء من روحي وقلمي وكياني.

لقد صنعتُها اليوم خصيصاً كي تساعدني على الكتابة، وحملتُها معي كالعادة لزيارة الأزرق العجوز، أنيسي ونيسي منذ الصغر، البحر.

آه يا بحر غزة.

البحر الذي حلمتُ منذ طفولتي أن أسكن بجواره. تحقَّق حلمي أخيراً، لكن مع فارق أنني جئتُه نازحاً، هارباً، تاركاً كل شيء خلفي، جئتُه باكياً أحمل في صدري دموع الكون، جئتُه عاتباً عليه:

"لماذا تستقبلني في ظروف كهذه؟"

"لماذا تدعوني بقربك تحت الطائرات المسيّرة والصواريخ، وليس تحت الطيور وضوء الشمس؟"

أدركتُ قبل أن أحتدَّ معه في الكلام أنه مثلي. أو ربما أنا مثله،

كلانا يعاني، وكلٌّ على طريقته.

جلستُ في حضرته صامتاً أتأمّلُه، أفكّرُ في بيتي الذي تركتُه.

أفكّرُ في بُعدي عن الأهل والأحباب والأصحاب، أفكّرُ في العم والخال، ومع تفكيري بهم مرّوا جميعهم أمام عينيّ؛ خالاتي وأخوالي وأعمامي وزوجاتهم وأبناؤهم وبناتهم الذين غادرونا فجأة، ومضوا.

لم يغادرونا برفق.

غادرونا بكلِّ قسوة. انتُزعوا منا بوحشية، بصاروخ حاقد من طائرة حاقدة تحملُ طياراً حاقداً مثلهما أو أشد حقداً.

ثلاثون روحاً أو أكثر.

انتشلناهم من تحت الأنقاض أشلاء.

اختلطت لحومُ الرجال مع لحوم النساء والأطفال.

ثلاثة أيام ونحن نلملمُ شتات أجسادهم من الأرض، ومن تحت الأرض، ومن فوق أسطح منازل الجيران.

ثم كانت المعجزة، معجزة جلبت الفرحة للجميع، وفي الوقت نفسه ضاعفت الألم.

طفلٌ واحد فقط بقي حيّاً، ابن خالي.

أخبروه أن أهله بخير. أخبرهم أنه رأى أباه يتناثر.

اطمأنَّ عندما رأى أمّه في العناية المركزة، كلَّمها وكلَّمته، لكن الفرحة العابرة اختفت من عينيه عندما لحقت أمّه بأبيه.

دعا الله أن تكون أخته الصغيرة بخير.

أخبروه أنها استشهدت مع والدهم في الليلة ذاتها.

أيُّ قلب قد يتحمَّل هذا الألم؟

بكيتُ بكلِّ حرقة أمام صبر هذا الصغير على هذه الفجائع المتلاحقة.

متُّ مع أبيه – خالي – وأمّه وأخته ألف ميتة، وأنا أرى براءة الطفولة تختفي شيئاً فشيئاً من هذا الوجه الصغير.

صبي لم يتجاوز الثانية عشرة من العمر، وقد شاخ قلبُه حتى كأنه على مشارف الأربعين.

مسحتُ دموعي التي انهمرت على هذه الذكرى كالمطر، ثم ما لبثَتْ أن تَبعَتْها ذكرى أخرى لعائلة هربت من بيتها خوفاً من القصف والموت. العائلة بأكملها أُبيدت، فيما بقي البيت واقفاً، كما هو، لم يُصبه شيء من أي شيء.

أنامُ وأصحو على أشدّ الذكرياتِ وطأةً على قلبي، فأودُّ أن أنامَ ولا أصحو أبداً.

كلُّ ذكرياتي أمام الأزرق العجوز كانت فيما مضى بالنسبة لي رائعة، مفعمة بالوجوه الحية التي أحببتها.

الآن، أجلسُ معه وحدي، فنجان قهوتي مترعٌ بالفقد، ومزيدٍ من الفقد، وفقدٍ غائرٍ عميق.

نعم، أعرفُ أن الحروبَ وقعت، وتقع، وستظلُّ تقع في العالم بأسره، وأن الموت الوحشي فعل بشريٌّ قبيح.

أعرفُ تماماً، كما حفَّظونا ونحن صغار، بأنَّ الدنيا بأكملها إلى زوال.

نعم، أنا أؤمن بذلك رغم كل شيء.

لكن أتعلمون أين مأساتي الخاصة في كل ما يحدث على هذه البقعة من الأرض؟

جرحي الأكبر، ذاك الذي يشقّ صدري؟

بعد أنْ ودَّعتُ زوجتي ودفنتُها بيديَّ هاتين، لا أستطيعُ أن أناديها باسمها الآن.

أخافُ أن أنادي عليها فلا تجيبني، فأصدّقُ حينها أنها رحلت.

تركتني ومضت.

رحلت كما رحل كثيرون قبلها.

الأزرق العجوز كان ثالثنا في لحظاتنا الجميلة معاً. في صمته، يعرف مقدار الألم الذي أعانيه. لا أعرف ما إذا كنتُ سأستطيع تحمُّله.

أنا وحدي الآن يا صديقي القديم.

عدتُ إليكَ كما كنتُ، لا أحد في حياتي غيرك أنتَ، وكلماتي، وقهوتي.

لكنني هذه المرة، عدتُ لأصبحَ مثلك.

روحٌ زرقاء شائخة.

محيطٌ شاسعٌ من الصمت.

كل يوم

ريما أبو موسى

عائدةٌ من مشوار عبثي ومُرهق، دون أن أجدَ وسيلة مواصلات إلى مفترق العودة في مدينة رفح، مضطرَّة أن أكمل الكيلومترين المتبقّيين مشياً.

أتاني صوتُ أمي على الموبايل:

- وينك يمّى؟ الحمد لله هناك إشارة للموبايل، صار لي ساعتين برن عليكِ، خفت يكون صار إلك إشي لا سمح الله!

- والله بهدلة مواصلات، ربنا اللي بعلم فيها.

- طيب يمّى أغربت الدنيا . . . خلصي بسرعة ورَوْحي.

كنتُ أتأمَّل وجوه المارة، واحداً تلو الآخر، بالبؤس الجامح الذي استوطن ملامحهم، يسيرون ذاهلين، كأنهم وجدوا أنفسهم ارتموا فجأة من عالمهم الطبيعي والمألوف، البشري جداً، إلى عالم كابوسي. في الوقت الذي كان من المُفترض أن أتجهَّز فيه لحفل تخرجي من كلية الصيدلة، ها أنا لم أعد أنتظر اليوم التالي أو اللحظة الآتية.

صوت أمّي ما زال على الموبايل:

- ألووو! معي؟

- معك يمّى معك . . . هَيْني في الطريق.

أخبرتُها بألا تقلق، ووعدتُها بأن أكون حذرة، وأنهينا المكالمة.

علت أصوات صاخبة في الشارع المعفَّر، طغى عليها صوت سائق عربة يجرُّها حمار، يصيح: "ضَهْرك.. ضَهْرك"، متحاشيةً، كما الناس من حوالي، الاصطدام بها. وبعد أن قطعتُ ما يقارب نصف ساعة من المشي، وقفت حافلة نقل صغيرة مُتهالكة كانت تُستخدم لنقل البضائع قبل أن تتحول، كأحد إملاءات الإبادة علينا، إلى نقل الرُّكاب.

سألني السائق عن وجهتي، فأجبتُه:

- مفترق العودة.

أشار لي بيده وقال:

- اركبي!

فتح أحد الركاب باب الحافلة جانبياً. صُدمت للمنظر. كان البشر مكدَّسين في كل فراغ متاح. سألتُ فاغرةً فمي:

- وين بدّي أركب؟

خطر لي في البداية أن أتراجع عن الركوب، لكنني نفضتُ الفكرة جانباً عندما فكّرتُ أنني قد لا أجد وسيلة نقل أخرى. حاولتُ أن أبدو أقل ارتباكاً وأقل تسبُّباً في الإزعاج والتأفُّف، وأنا أتابع الرُّكاب وهم يحاولون أن يفسحوا لي مكاناً لأجلسَ فيه. لم يجدوا سوى مساحة ضيقة بين طفلة في العاشرة من عمرها، على كرسيّ متحرك، بُترت ساقها، وقد غشى الذهولُ وجهَها كأنها كانت ترى كابوساً، وبين رجلٍ خمسينيّ، ذاب خجلاً وهو يلملمُ نفسه لئلا يحتكّ لحمُه بلحمي.

انطلقت الحافلة، تنهبُ عجلاتُها الواهنة الطريقَ المشحون بالتوجُّس والاحتمالات غير المطمئنة. نَقَّلتُ عيني بين وجوه الركاب، ممَّن كانوا في مرمى نظري. كان هناك قاسم مشترك بينها جميعاً: الأسى.

جلست قبالتي أمٌّ تحاول أن تُسكِت طفلَها الذي كان يلحُّ على شيء لم أعرف ما هو، فيما بدت عاجزةً عن تلبية طلبه. إلى جانبها امرأة عجوز كانت تتحسبن* على من أوصلنا إلى هذه الحال، وفي مؤخرة الحافلة شباب تركّز حديثهم الساخط على الغلاء والاحتكار الذي نشهده.

توقفت الحافلة فجأة. صاح بنا السائق:

- يلا يا جماعة، مفترق كير.. كلُّه ينزل، بدي ألفّ وأرجع.

قلتُ له، فيما كان الركاب يهمّون بالنزول وهم صامتون:

- أنا مش نازلة هان، أنا نازلة عند مفترق العودة يا عمّ.

أجابني السائق بنزق، كما لو كان يُفترض أن أكون على دراية بالوضع العام:

- مفترق العودة زحمة، كمليها مشي.. كلها خطوتين.

لم يكن أمامي خيار، ثم إنَّ جميع الركاب نزلوا دون أن يحتجَّ أحد، فقلتُ له بيأس:

- توكّل على الله!

ترجّلتُ، وأكملتُ الطريق سيراً، وأنا أدمدم: "الله يلعن أبو المواصلات، على أبو الطريق، على أبو الناس، على أبو الإبادة، على أبو الحياة! يا شيخة!"

صرتُ كما المجنونة أكلِّمُ نفسي وأنا أسير: "'خطوتين'؟! 'خطوتين' يا عمّ؟! كل هذه المسافة 'خطوتين'؟! في أي عُرف يصبح الكيلومتران خطوتين؟! بكرة بنصير نقطع البلد كلها مشي. ما هي كلها قديش؟! خطوتين!".

وصلتُ البيت بعد نصف ساعة. ما إن دخلت، حتى هتفتُ من الجوع:

---

*أي تتلفظ بجملة "حسبنا الله ونعم الوكيل".

- وينك يمّى؟! وين الغدا؟ شو طابخة؟

جاء ردُّ أمي أقرب إلى توبيخ:

- هيك الواحد بحكي؟

ثم قالت بنبرة استسلام:

- فاصوليا ورز.

لم أكن أحبُّ هذه "الطبخة" التي أصبحت طبقاً رسمياً في واقعنا الجديد الكئيب. ولم نكن ندري أن هذه الطبخة ستغدو قريباً ترفاً وذكرى مشتهاة، حين سيصبح أي شيء قابلاً للأكل حتى وإن لم يُخلق لذلك.

تابعتُ أمي فيما كانت تُقسِّم حصص الطعام لكل صحن، حسب عددنا، موجهةً كلامها لي:

- باقي رغيفين من الخبز. كُلي واحد وخلي لأختك آلاء واحد.

كانت آلاء مصابة باضطراب طيف التوحُّد، ولم تكن تستطيع أن تأكل أي شيء يوضع على الطاولة، إذ طوّرت انتقائيةً شديدة تجاه الطعام، معتادةً على وجبات بعينها. آخر مرة نفد فيها لدينا مخزوننا من الطحين، بكت منتحبةً وكأننا لا نريد إطعامها. إنّ مفردات مثل: نفاد الطحين، وطابور الكوبونات الغذائية، وحصّة الفرد، والانتظار، والصبر، ومحاولة إيجاد البديل، والطوارئ، وشحّ الموارد، حتى الإبادة، كلها كانت بعيدة عن فهمها. وكانت أمي تسعى جاهدة لتُخصِّص لها الأكل الذي يتلاءم مع حالتها الصحية. لم نشأ أن نفكِّر بما قد يحدث لاحقاً، نافضين من رؤوسنا أيَّ احتمال بألا يكون هناك طعام لها من الأساس.

كنتُ متعبة، أجرجرُ قدمي بصعوبة. قلتُ لأمي:

- اطلبي من حدا من خواتي تحضِّر لي الأكل عبال ما أصلي عشان أنام، ولا حدا يصحيني!

ردَّت عليّ بغضب:

- هُوي إنتِ قاعدة في فندق؟! انقلعي من وجهي!

هذا مشهد صغير أعيش معاناته كل يوم، اسمه "المواصلات." تحولت حياتنا إلى حالة ركض دائم لتأمين مقومات الحياة الأساسية.

كنتُ قد ركبتُ في الصباح مع مجموعة من النسوة والشباب على عربة يجرُّها حمار، للذهاب إلى منطقة بعيدة للحصول على كوبونة غذائية. وعدتُ في نهاية اليوم لا أحمل شيئاً معي إلا الغضب، يغلي الدم في عروقي من السخط والنقمة، حتى شعرتُ بالنار تكاد تشتعل في كياني، لتحرقَ العالمَ من حولي.

من أين جاءت كلمة "كوبونة"؟ فكرت. إنّها كلمة جديدة، تسلَّلت إلى قاموسنا نحنُ الغزيين، كلمة نعرفها جميعنا، تتردَّد على ألسنة صغيرنا قبل كبيرنا، أسمعُها عشرات المرات في اليوم الواحد. سطت علينا. احتلَّتْنا. هي أول شيء نفتح عليه وعيَنا في الصباح، وآخر شيء نختم به حياتَنا في المساء.

وضعتُ رأسي على الوسادة، أخطِّط لمشوار غد؛ إذ اتفقتُ مع صديقة لي، من الكلية، كي نذهب معاً للحصول على كوبونات غذائية من مركز توزيع على بعد ساعة مشياً.

ككل يوم، يبدأ زحفُ الفلسطينين نحو طوابير الكوبونات في الفجر. ينطلقون بأجساد متداعية وأرواح مستنزفة وعيون واجمة، مفتوحة على اتساع؛ زومبيات في طريقهم إلى قيامتهم.

اسمه سلام

خلود أبو ظاهر

الساعة الثالثة فجراً. تجلسُ بزاوية شبة قائمة، تستندُ إلى وسادة داكنة اللون تشبه الغد، يؤنسها صوتُ الصمت الجلي. ملامحُها متورّمة، شاحبة، بهالات سوداء حول عينيها. وجهُها يتصبَّبُ عرقاً. قدماها المتشقِّقتان تعلوان فرشاً مرتَّقاً، يشبه الحالة العامة.

يلازمُها من الجانب الأيسر زوجُها الذي يوقظه رذاذُ الحبّ والحدس الكامن في ثنايا الروح. عيناه تحدِّقان من دون أن ترمشا، وبنظرة سريعة فاحصة يقول لها:

- يبدو أن الوقت حان، ماذا بمقدوري أن أفعل؟!

تجيبُه بصوت حاد، متحشرج:

- أريدُ أمي.

ترقُّ تدريجياً، وتمتلئُ مقلتاها بالدموع، ويعمُّ الصمت.

تسيطرُ عليه مشاعر ملتبسةً، مردِّداً بأسى:

- ألا تعلمين أن أمك مازالت محاصرة في مدينة غزة؟ وقدومها لمناطق الجنوب حيث نحن ليس بالأمر الهين؟!

هنا يلاطفُها بقبلة دافئة على خدِّها الأيسر؛ ليس بالضرورة أن تخفِّفَ آلامَ المخاض، كما لا تعوضها عن غياب الأم، لكن هذا هو الاحتواء الذي يقدر عليه.

قُبلتُه تُحفِّزها لتقفَ منتصبةً وسط الخيمة، وتلملمَ بقايا النصائح العالقة بجدار الذاكرة علَّها تكون كافية لولادة طفلها الأول. ورغم اقتراب وقت الخلاص، تتأوَّه بصمت. يشتدُّ الألم، تارَّة تضعُ يدَها خلف ظهرها، وتارَّة أخرى تميلُ بوهن على دعامة الخيمة ركيكة البناء، وتارَّة ثالثة تصرخ دون أن يسمعها أحد، وعشرات المرات تلعن مشاعر الأمومة في بلاد ثائرة، كل شيء فيها لا يتسنّى له أن يكبر، ثم يكبر، ويكبر أكثر، قبل أن يموت.

ما بين ركلة حياة وأخرى ثلاثون دقيقة، وقتٌ كافٍ لتتحسَّس فيه إبطيها وما يجب تفقُّده من جسدها، "أوه . . . الشعيرات نبتت مجدداً، حان وقت إزالتها"، تُتمتم بينها وبين نفسها.

تنهض متثاقلة، تفتِّش بين حقائبها المركونة في طرف الخيمة عن شفرة حلاقة نسائية، بديلاً يفي بالغرض عن السكر "المطبوخ" باهظ الثمن، والمحارم المعطَّرة بديلاً عن الماء الشحيح.

تتفقَّد بعدها حقيبة المولود؛ ملابس صيفية في شهر ديسمبر، تنمُّ عن عبثيّة الحياة، جُلّها مستعملة والبقية منها تبرعات، وفوطتان نسائيتان مصنوعتان يدوياً من بقايا الأقمشة ذات اللون الداكن، وحفاضتان. كل هذا جعلها تشعر بالخجل من استقبال غير محتفى به للمولود.

شمس الصباح، متقلِّبة المزاج في الشتاء، تقتحمُ الخيمة البائسة، فتجفِّف بقايا الندى العالق على سقفها المصنوع من غطاء من النايلون السميك. تشعر بأن النهار يمدُّ لها طوق نجاة من ولادة ليلية قد تُكلِّفها حياتها، أو حياة المولود، أو كلاهما معاً.

الألم الآن يعلن شراسته. مع تسارع المخاض، يتعين اختيار وسيلة نقل إلى المستشفى؛ عربة يجرُّها حمار أو حصان أو "توك توك"، بثمن ليس زهيداً، وبشروط يقرِّرُها صاحبُ العربة أو السائق. يقع الخيار على عربة يجرُّها حصان، كونها الأنسب للوضع الحالي.

ما إن تنجو من زحام المارة بعد سنوات وهميَّة من الانتظار، حتى تقع مجدداً في فخ زحام المصابين والقتلى والمرضى بين أزقة المستشفى. لم يكن زحاما عادياً. كل شيء هنا مبعثر؛ الإنسان وكرامته، الأمان، الاطمئنان، الحب، كل شيء . . . كل شيء.

تصفن فجأة. يسكن ألم المخاض متضامناً مع هول المنظر. صلاة جنازة تُقام على مجموعة أكياس تضمُّ أشلاء، وأكفان متراصة، بينهم طفل رضيع موشَّح بالأبيض. بحركة تلقائية، تضعُ يدَها على بطنها، تتفقَّدُ جنينَها وتمضي قلقة.

الدماء تلوِّث كل شيء. هنا، تشعر أنه من العيب أن يكون لون الورد والحب أحمر. على ضيقها، تفيضُ الممرات بأجساد جراحها مفتوحة على الملأ. الأطباء والعاملون والناس جميعهم في حالة ركض متواصل. صفارات سيارات الإسعاف لا تتوقف أبداً، تصاحبُ كلَّ صوت انفجار.

تلتفتُ على صوت أحدهم يصرخ فيها قائلاً:

- عليكِ التوجُّه إلى قسم الولادة، فقد أصبح في المبنى الخلفي من المستشفى. المبنى الأمامي مخصص لاستقبال الجرحى والقتلى.

تتمتمُ مجدَّداً: "يا إلهي متى سينتهي هذا اليوم الطويل؟".

تتَّكئُ على كتف زوجها، فيما تخطو بثقل، تصعدُ السُّلمَ درجةً، درجةً، قبل أن تصل أخيراً غرفة الولادة.

ترى أمامها جهاز تخطيط نبضات القلب، وما يلزم من معدات الولادة الطبيعية، وأسِرَّة حديدية تفصل فيما بينها ستائر بيضاء، تحجب الرؤية لا الصوت، ولا ملابسات وظروف كل حالة ولادة؛ طفل يُولد لأب شهيد يحمل اسمه، وأم لا تنفك تردِّد: "لا أريد أن ألد وأنا نازحة في الخيام"، وأخرى تجهش بالبكاء لا تدري فرحةً أم استياء، وجدَّة تقف عند الباب تهلِّل مبتهجةً لولادة حفيدها، الذكر الأول بعد خمس بنات.

تعتلي سريرها. يخوضُ طفلُها حالة العراك الأخير من أجل الحياة التي يظن أنها شيء ثمين يستحق التشبُّث به.

يتضاعفُ الألم أكثر فأكثر، ركلة تلو الأخرى، ينتفضُ جسدها في كل ركلة، وتنقبضُ عضلات وجهها من شدة الوجع. يحثُّها الطبيب مراراً وتكراراً: "هيا . . . شهيق، زفير . . . شهيق، زفير . . . لم يتبقَ سوى القليل، ادفعي . . . ادفعي".

ثم صرخة، صوت حياة جديدة، صوت جديد، صوت يُصرُّ على الحياة رغم كل شيء. وجه مستدير، بشرة بيضاء تميل للحمرة وكأنها ممزوجة بالحناء، شعر أسود، عينان بنيّتان واسعتان، شفاه وردية، وجنتان حمراوان، كأنه رسول مُبشّر بحتمية البقاء.

يمازحُها الطبيب مبتسماً:

- ماذا ستُسمين هذا الصغير المشاكس؟

تجيبُ متنهِّدة:

- سلام . . . سأسمّيه سلام.

معروف

غسان سلام

ككُل ليالي البرد القارسة، كانت هذه الليلة عارية، إلا من عتمة قاتمة، كأن لا نهاية لها. لا وقت يمرُّ، والموتُ يحلقُ فوقك من كل اتجاه.

الحرب ظالمة، تنهشُ أرواحَنا، وتسلبُنا أحلامَنا، وتسلخُنا من جلدنا، وتطردُنا من ذواتنا، فنتيه في أجسادنا، ونصبحُ غرباء حتى عن أنفسنا التي كنّا نعرفها.

تشعرُ أنك في سباق مع حتفك وأنتَ تحاولُ الخلاص، تختلقُ خطواتٍ من الوهم كي لا توصد الأرض أبوابها أمامك، ولكن سرعان ما تسقط أمام عجزك. أيُّ صلابة لها أن تثبتَ أمام القهر؟ أيُّ إنسانٍ يستطيع أن يتوارى من الموت؟

ما زلتُ أعيش كل لحظة من أيامي كأنها تلك الليلة؛ ليلة النزوح من بيتنا في خان يونس إلى ضجيج الخوف والرعب. خرجتُ من دون وداع لأي شيء، فلفظني كلُّ ما كنتُ أعرفه، وكأنني ابن العراء.

شعرتُ أنني أعمى أمام هول ما رأيت، وكأن عينيَّ لا تريدان أن تصدقا، وقد آثرتا أن تبدلا نورهما بالسواد على ألا يُذبحَ قلبي. ولكن لا مفر، فحواسي كلها استيقظت.

لا وقتَ للراحة أو الانسحاب من المشهد، فكل ما فيك يجب أن يكونَ شاهداً على ما حدث. كيف لهذا كلّه أن يحدث؟ لم نحن بالتحديد؟

ثقيلة جداً هذه المأساة، أثقل منّا، ومن مجموع مآسينا.

كنتُ أحاولُ الاختباء من نيران الاحتلال داخل بيت دفيئة، غطاؤه الخارجي من البلاستيك الشفاف، وكانت أمامنا أرضٌ خلاء، معالمها لم تكن واضحة بسبب

الظلام. ورغم صوت القصف المدوي والغارات المزلزلة من حولنا وأزيز الطائرات المسيَّرة المتواصل، سمعتُ صوتَ بكاء طفل من جهة الأرض الخلاء.

شعرتُ بقلبي يخرجُ من مكانه، وبيديَّ تطيران نحو الصغير تُطبطبان عليه، وتمتدّان إليه كي تنتشلاه. لكنَّ السماء كانت في أوج غضبها، وكأنها تصبُّ سخطَها علينا لتمنعنا من أي وصلٍ كان له بالإمكان أن يكون.

كانت الطائرات الحربية تنيرُ ما حولنا، ليس نوراً وإنما نار، أضاء لهيبُها المتصاعد المشهد؛ عائلة تتألف من رجل وامرأة وطفلين، أحدهما استلقى إلى جوار أبيه، والآخر في حضن أمِّه، التي على الأرجح كانت تركض هاربة، تحمل صغيرها إلى صدرها، حتى إذا سقطت على الأرض وقد اخترقت قذيفة ظهرها، ظلَّ طفلها محصَّناً في حضنها، ذراعاها – هي القتيلة – تلتفّان حوله. كان يبكي، مستجدياً أمه، لكنها كانت صامتة. صوت بكائه اخترق قلبي.

حاولتُ التحرك، لكنني كنتُ أقرب لأن أكونَ هدفاً للموت. خشيتُ على الطفل من ذهابي نحوه، فقد نُقتل كلانا. ربما أستطيع، لعلَّني أتمكّن من إنقاذه، لا أريدُ لهذه الفرصة أن تموت. كانت أصواتُ القصف تتعالى، وبكاء الطفل تارةً يعلو، وتارةً يخفت. كلما علا بكاؤه، شعرتُ ببعض الأمل. وكلما سكن، جلدتُ نفسي بسياط اللوم حتى شعرتُ وكأنَّ أنفاسي تَقطَّعت.

ساعة، ساعتان، ثلاث. ثقلت جفوني، وتعب أنينُ الطفل، فحلَّ الصمتُ حتى أيقظتني الشمس. أخيراً خلع الليلُ رعبَه، وإن بقيت ظلمتُه ماثلةً في قرار روحي.

كنتُ مرهقاً، وجلاً، لكن قلبي دفعني بقوة حتى وصلتُ مكانَ العائلة. لم يستيقظ منهم أحد، ولا حتى الصغير، اقتربتُ كي أتَفقَّدهم، ربما استقبلتهم الشمس أيضاً، لكنني وجدتهم غارقين في ظلام الأمس، غارقين في الدم، غارقين في الموت.

ما هي إلا لحظات حتى عادت الطائرات الإسرائيلية تحتلُّ السماء. شعرتُ كأن كرة صوف كبيرة تلتفُّ خيوطها العريضة حول رأسي، فأغلقتُ عينيَّ، وكتمتُ أنفاسي، ثم امتدَّت الكرة داخل فمي فخنقتْ صوتي. أحسستُ بدمي متحجِّراً وجسدي مشلولاً، أقفُ عاجزاً، واهن القوى.

كانت الهزيمة تحكم قبضتها عليّ، وقد ظننتُ أنني استسلمت، حين ارتفع بكاء الطفل فجأة. سرت قشعريرةٌ هائلةٌ في جسدي، أذابت جمودَه، وحلّت كرة الصوف. دفقت الدماءُ في أطرافي، وتسارعت أنفاسي، وتحرَّرتُ من خوفي. كان عقلي في قدمي، كان سريعاً ومغامراً، لأول مرَّة لم أره يتردَّد، بل كان ثابتاً، يعرف هدفه جيداً، كان كالصقر.

انتشلتُ الرضيع، الذي لعلّه تجاوز عامه الأول، من حضن أمه، وانطلقتُ مبتعداً عن المكان بسرعة. لم أنظر إليه، كنتُ أرفع بصري إلى السماء، أحاول أن أرصد طائرة قد تستهدفنا معاً، دون أن يحيد بصري عن الطريق أمامي. لا أعرفُ كم مضى من الوقت حتى وصلتُ إلى بيتٍ قد يحمينا، أنا والصغير، وإن لم تكن سماؤه آمنة، ككل سماوات غزة وسقوفها. كان بيتاً من الواضح أنه فارغ من أهله منذ وقت ليس ببعيد. عاينتُ أرجاء البيت كسارقٍ اعتدى على حُرمة المكان. أخيراً تسنّى لي أن أرى الصغير. ما إن وقعت عيناي عليه حتى سرق قلبي. كان نائماً كالملاك، لا بل كالأطفال كما يجب أن يناموا بسلام، كأنه وردةٌ من قطنٍ ناعم، مزروعةٌ في حقل من الطمأنينة، لا يدري أنهم اقتلعوا جذوره.

والآن ماذا سأفعل؟ سألتُ نفسي. استدرتُ حولي باحثاً عن أي شيء. فكّرتُ أن أضع الطفلَ على فراش، لكنني تردَّدتُ، أو بالأحرى خفتُ عليه، فهو الآن في عهدتي. بدأت أتحرك بقلب أم، اتجهتُ نحو المطبخ، فوجدتُ على الطاولة بقايا طعام قد تسدُّ رمقَ جوعي. لكن من الآن فصاعداً، هناك معدة بحجم بيضة يجب أن تمتلئ أولاً. فتَّشتُ في غرف البيت عن أي شيء يمكن أن يأكله الطفل. ثم عدتُ إلى المطبخ لأبحث في الخزائن والثلاجة عن حليب. وجدتُ بعضَ الأعشاب، فغليتُ اليانسون. أعتقد أن رائحته دغدغت أنفَ الكائن الصغير وأيقظتْه. حاولتُ تبريد المشروب سريعاً، لكن كيف سأناوله إياه؟ قمتُ بالبحث أكثر في محتويات المطبخ، فوجدتُ كيساً يحتوي على حُقن للسوائل. كان ذلك الحل الوحيد.

بدأتُ أعطيه المشروب بالحقنة، وأنا أراقبُ وجهه. أصابع يده الصغيرة التفَّت حول إصبعي. ما هذا؟ إحساس لم أختبره من قبل تغلغل في داخلي بدفء وعذوبة، حتى نسيتُ الوقت ونسيتُ الخوف.

لم يكن هناك شيء آخر أستطيع أن أقدّمه للكائن الصغير. كان يتعيَّن عليَّ مغادرة البيت بسرعة، فكلُّ بيت في غزة منتصب البنيان كان هدفاً للفتك به.

خرجتُ من البيت، أحضن الطفل قريباً من قلبي، يتدلى من يدي كيسٌ به بضع ملابس حملتُها من البيت، معتذراً لأهل البيت في سرّي.

مشيتُ مسرعاً، فيما غفا الصغير بين ذراعي. وصلتُ إلى مكان فيه ناس يشبهونني. كنا جميعاً نعيش الصدمة ذاتها، ونحمل ملامح التعب نفسها.

توجهتُ نحو مدرسة للإيواء. لم تكن هناك صفوف قادرة على استقبال المزيد من النازحين، فاحتللتُ بقعةً صغيرةً تأوينا، أنا وصغيري، في ساحة المدرسة. تم تسجيل اسمي كنازح، وسُجِّل الطفل، الذي لا أعرف اسمه أو عائلته، كيتيم مجهول النسب، بناء على شهادتي على وفاة عائلته. طُلِبَ مني أن أمنحه اسماً مبدئياً ليُسجَّل به. عندها، أصابتني حالة غريبة من الضحك؛ الضحك الهستيري الذي يكتمُ خلفه غصَّة. فكرتُ قليلاً من باب تحمُّلي مسؤوليته، هذه المسؤولية التي توليتُها منذ يوم واحد فقط. أجبت: "معروف. سأسميه معروف".

مرَّ يومان قبل أن أتمكن من الوصول إلى عائلتي، إذ افترقنا أثناء النزوح، شتَّتنا العدو، وجعلَنا مبعثرين، كلٌّ يبحثُ عن خلاصه.

وجدتهم في مدرسة إيواء أخرى، ولحسن الحظ هذه المرة كانوا قد حصلوا على نصف مساحة صف مدرسي. كانوا ينتظرونني بفارغ الصبر، واستقبلونا، أنا ومعروف، بكل حفاوة، بعد أن علموا بقصته.

اختارت أختي أن تعتني بصغيري إلى حين معرفة أي خبر عن أهله. ولكن اجتياح خان يونس طال، ولم يكن أحد يستطيع الرجوع إلى المدينة. كنت أعُدُّ الأيام للعودة إلى بيتي مع أسرتي. ورغم قسوة الحياة، فقد ملأها معروف بخفَّة روحه.

انتهى الاجتياح في شهر إبريل 2024. كم كان الخبر مفرحاً، وكم كان ثقيلاً على قلبي. لم أعُد كالجميع أتفقَّدُ بيتَنا، عدتُ أتفقد مسرحَ الجريمة.

وصلتُ إلى البقعة التي انتشلتُ منها معروف. بدأتُ أتَعَرَّق، وشعرتُ بالتنميل في يديّ. اختنقت. لم يكن هناك هواء أبتلعه. من جديد، استدرجتني مشاعر الخوف والرعب، فسقطتُ فيها عميقاً. كان هناك بقايا أشلاء وهياكل عظمية. حمدتُ الله أن أحداً لم يسبقني إلى المكان. وجدتُ ملابس متناثرة، فتَّشتُها،

فوجدتُ فيها أوراقاً ثبوتية. قلَّبتُها بيدين مرتجفتين. كانت تخصُّ عائلة معروف.

وأخيراً معروف سوف يصبحُ معروفاً. قرأتُ أسماء أفراد عائلته، ثم طويتُ الأوراق ووضعتُها في جيبي وعدتُ إلى مدرسة الإيواء ملتحقاً أنا ومعروف بأسرتي. معروف كان آدم. كان الأصل كله، فكيف جعلوه مجهولاً؟

ظللتُ أسبوعاً أتجنَّب مناقشة أي أمر له علاقة بمعروف، إلى أن تحدَّث أبي معي بشأن ضرورة البحث عمَّن تبقى من عائلته وإعادته لهم. لماذا يا أبي؟ لماذا تُعلِّق قلبي على حبل المشنقة؟

لكن هذا ما يجب القيام به. استجمعتُ قواي، وبدأتُ بالسؤال عن العائلة الممتدة، هل هناك جدّ أو عمّ، أو أقارب من الدرجة الثانية؟

بعد عشرة أيام استطعتُ التواصل مع عمّ الصغير. لم يُصدق. كاد الرجلُ يُجن. وأخيراً وجد أثراً من أخيه.

وأنا؟ ماذا سيتبقى لي بعد معروف؟ لقد احتلَّ جزءاً كبيراً مني ومن أيامي. جاء أهله لاستلامه. كان صغيراً لاستيعاب ما يحدث، وأنا أيضاً كنتُ أصغر من أن أتلقى كل هذا الألم.

مرَّت ثلاثة أشهر على رحيل طفلي. كنتُ أتصفح الهاتف حين وقع بصري على خبر قصف البيت الذي كان يعيش فيه آدم مع أسرة عمّه. لم أتمالك نفسي من الخوف. هرعتُ إلى المكان سريعاً؟ ما الذي فعلتُه؟ لمتُ نفسي غاضباً. هل ساعدتُه في النجاة كي أُلقيه في فم الموت مرة أخرى؟ يا ليتني لم أفعل!

وصلتُ إلى موقع القصف. شعرتُ بالنهاية؛ كأنّ يداً أطبقت على عنقي. آآآآه! لماذا يا الله؟ لماذا؟

كان مسعفون من الدفاع المدني ينتشلون الجثث والإصابات. عرفتُه من أصابع قدميه، لقد قبَّلتُها كثيراً. أعرفُ هاتين القدمين المنمنمتين جيداً. وجدتُني معه داخل سيارة الإسعاف. كان معروف على قيد الحياة، لكنه مصاب. شكرتُ الله وأجهشتُ بالبكاء.

لازمتُه طيلة مكوثه في المستشفى، لم يتبقَّ أحدٌ من عائلة عمّه. جميع من كانوا بالبيت قُتلوا، وعاش ابن قلبي.

عادت إليَّ الحياة من جديد. عاد الصباح. عادت الأوقاتُ كلها. عاد إليَّ معروف، إلى حين. بعد ستة أشهر، ظهر رقم غير مسجل على موبايلي. شيءٌ في قلبي وقع.

- ألو؟

- نعم.

- الأخ سامي؟

- نعم، من يُحدثني؟

- نعيمة، عمَّة الطفل آدم.

ماذا؟! من أين خرجتِ، إنه لم يعد آدم، إنه معروف، هذه المرة لن يستطيع أحد انتزاعه مني. تابعتُ حديثي معها، دون أن أتمكن من تخفيف نبرة العصبية في صوتي:

- لا أعرف أنَّ للطفل عمَّة على قيد الحياة.

- أنا في جباليا، شمال غزة، وعلمتُ منذ قرابة الشهر بنجاة ابن أخي، وأنه في عهدتك.

- حسناً، والآن ما هو المطلوب؟

- سوف آخُذه.

حاولتُ أنْ ألجم غضبي، قائلاً:

- لكن لا توجد طرق مفتوحة بين الشمال والجنوب.

كنتُ أحاول إبعاد الفكرة من رأسها، فأجابتني بهدوء وإصرار:

- سوف ننتظر حتى أستطيع الوصول لآدم.

لم ينقضِ أسبوعان حتى تم الاتفاق على هدنة، وفُتحت الطرق؛ كأن العالم تواطأ عليَّ كي يسلبني طفلي.

جاءت العمَّة، وأخذت معروف. هذه المرة أنا وأهلي لم نعد بخير، فقد صنع معروف البهجة والحب في حياتنا، وتعلَّقت أرواحُنا به، بعدما أصبح طفل العائلة.

بعد أقل من شهرين عاد العدوان الإسرائيلي، أكثر همجيةً ووحشية، وتكالبت الهمومُ أكثر فأكثر. أصبحت تفصلنا عن معروف مسافة أطول بكثير وأصعب للتنقل. كنتُ أتواصل معه عبر الفيديو باستخدام الموبايل، أخجل أن أعبِّر عن حبي واشتياقي له أمام عائلته، كما أخشى أن يشعر بخوفي وضعفي، هو الذي لم يعهد مني سوى الابتسامة والفرح.

بات ينطق كلمات أكثر الآن. في كل اتصال، كان يطلبُ أن آتي لرؤيته، وكنتُ أعده بذلك، لكنني كنتُ أعرف أنني لا أستطيع أن أفي بوعدي له. فكيف تشرح لطفلك أن ما يفصلك عنه ليس مسافة، وإنما موت بين موت وآخر؟

توالت الأحداث، وازدحمت الأيام، وتناقصت الحياة، لكنني كنتُ أهرب دائماً بأفكاري نحو طفلي، فأصبحُ طفلاً صغيراً يستطيعُ الكبار "خداعه" ومسايرته. هؤلاء الكبار هذه المرة أنا. كنتُ أخدع نفسي بالكلمات والأمنيات لأُخرِسَ فقدي.

كانت الساعة الواحدة بعد الظهر. ذهبتُ برفقة عدد من الأصدقاء إلى مقهى قريب، أحد الأماكن النادرة التي تتوفر فيها الكهرباء والإنترنت. تداولنا الكثير من الأخبار والقصص التي تحدث كل يوم ونكاد لا نصدِّقها. كنا جالسين على الطاولة نحتسي القهوة أمام شاشة التلفزيون، حين جاء خبر عاجل؛ فقد قصف الطيران الإسرائيلي مدينة جباليا في شمال غزة، وتم استهداف شخص على دراجة. كان هناك الكثير من الجرحى، والكثير من القتلى.

عاينتُ الجثث المتناثرة في الشارع عبر الشاشة. تفحّصت عيناي الوجوه. خفق قلبي وهو يسابقُ المشاهد المتتابعة في التلفزيون.

وجدتُه. نعم عرفتُه.

كيف لا أعرفه وقد حفظته عيناي؟ كيف لا أعرفه وبصمته محفورة في قلبي وروحه مجدولة بروحي؟

ذهبَ معروف، وبقيتُ أنا.

وأنا ذهبتُ، ولم أعُد.

رغوة الطريق

ديانا صليح

صببتُ صابوناً سائلاً أصفر في بطن كفّي اليُسرى التي اتّخذت تلقائياً شكل تجويف عميق، كبئرٍ يتوق ليعود بئراً.

كنتُ أحتاج إلى أن أغسل يديَّ بعد استخدام المرحاض المجاور لخيمتنا، لكن صنبور الماء غالباً ما يكون فارغاً. لقد أُبيد الماء كما أبيد الناس، حتى غدا شبحاً يتكرَّمُ علينا بالحضور، نركضُ وراءه، لا منه.

كان المرحاض البائس مشيَّداً من آربعة أعمدة خشبية، تلفُّها ستارةٌ مُرتجلة من قطعة قماش، ترقَّقت من الاهتراء، بحيث ترى ظلَّ من خلفها، في مسرحية هزلية فاضحة تُشبه ما نحن فيه، وبطانية مليئة بالثقوب وبُرادة الخشب وُضِعت لتؤدي دور الباب.

صُبَّ داخل المرحاض قالبٌ اسمنتي به دائرة في المنتصف. وكنتَ تحتاج إلى وقت لتقنع نفسك بدخول مكان كهذا، فما إن تتسلل الرائحة النفّاذة إلى أنفك حتى تُعتَصر جفونك، ويقبض عليك شعورٌ عارم بالغثيان.

فكَّرتُ بالذهاب إلى المرحاض العام اللعين، الأبعد. كنتُ أكره أن أذهب إليه في الأسابيع الأولى من نزوحنا، لكنه كان الوحيد في المنطقة الذي يمكن أن تقضي حاجتك فيه وتستحم من عفرات البؤس الطاغي في كل خلية هواء. وما كان يُغيظُني أنه هو الآخر بائس ورثّ، وجعله الازدحام أكثر رثاثةً وفُحشاً، مليئاً بالرمال وأوراق المراحيض والفوط الصحية، متناثرة في كل زاوية منه.

امتعضت مخيِّلتي من طقوس الذهاب إلى المرحاض العام للنساء الذي يبعد عن خيمتنا قرابة الخمسين متراً. "هل أذهب؟"، سألتُ نفسي بصوت عالٍ.

قرَّرتُ أن أذهب. وأخذتُ أتقدَّم خطوة، وأتراجعُ اثنتين. كنتُ أسألُ الغادي من المرحاض:

- هل توجد مياه في الصنبور اليوم؟

وكنتُ أستعدُّ لتلقي الإجابة التي أنتظرها بحماسة طفلة لقطعة حلوى:

- يتعين عليكِ الإسراع قبل أن تنفد المياه.

أو، الإجابة التي غالباً ما كنتُ أتوقعها:

- لا يوجد أي ماء!

فكنّا نضطرُّ جميعاً، نساءً ورجالاً وأطفالاً، إلى التسلُّح بزجاجة ماء بلاستيكية، في إعلان صريح بأننا "ذاهبون إلى المرحاض"، ونأخذ معنا فلقة صابون في علبة، وإن كان معظم الناس لا يكترثون لاستخدامها، إذ لم تكن تُحدِث أي رغوة، كأنك تغسل يديك بصخرة.

زفرتُ، ورفعتُ عينيَّ عن كفّي محملقةً في لا شيء يحدجني بلونه الرمادي، ثم خرجتُ إلى الطريق الرملي المقابل لمُخيَّم النازحين المتهالك الذي أقطن فيه، مخيَّم الكرامة، مع أنّ الكرامة تستغيث في هذه البُقعة المُتسخة والمُستهلكة، الغاصّة بالفوضى والركض المُستميت كي تبتلَّ العروق بجرعة حياة.

كان الطريق خالياً تماماً، إذ كان الوقت مبكراً في الصباح. وكانت الجلبة هاجعة في ذلك الوقت. ومع ذلك، لم أستطِع أن أُريح كتفيَّ كإشارة أخبر بها حواسي أننا وحيدون وآمنون. أبقيتُ أصابعي مغلقةً بإحكام حول سائل الجلي الأصفر، في وضعية جعلتُ فيها قبضةَ يدي مُعلَّقةً بموازاة جسدي في الجهة اليسرى، حريصةً على ألا ينسكب ما فيها.

قطعتُ الشوط كله نحو المرحاض، خطوةً خطوة، ومتراً متراً، وخيمةً خيمة، بالقاطنين فيها كما هم، لا يَتغيَّرون ولا يُغيِّرون نظراتهم الفضولية. مررتُ بمكبّ نفايات على شكل هلال، وقد فاض منه كل أنواع مُعلبات الطعام التي أتلفت جدران أمعائنا، وجعلتنا متَّحدين في الإخراج.

سال شيءٌ من راحتي، كخيط من الدماء تسرَّب بين أصابعي قبل أن يمتدَّ إلى رسغي، مشكِّلاً قطرات كانت تزداد كثافةً كلما تقدمتُ أكثر. ارتعشت يدي، وزاغت عيناي. أوهمتُ نفسي، دون أنْ أنظر، أنَّ ما يحدث ليس في يدي بل في عقلي. سرَّعتُ خطواتي، وأنا أرتجف، وأسمع خفقان قلبي.

أخيراً، وصلتُ إلى المرحاضين العامّين الوحيدين في المنطقة، أحدهما للنساء والآخر الرجال؛ كلاهما محاطان بغطاء بلاستيكي أبيض يحمل كلمة "يونيسيف" باللون الأزرق.

دخلتُ، وبدأتُ أستمع إلى "حكاوي الحمّام" التي لا تقلُّ رثاثةً عن رثاثة المرحاض نفسه، مختبرةً تعارفاً لا مثيل له بين نساء أمضين وقتاً طويلاً في طابور المرحاض، وعجائز يتشمَّتنَ بجيلنا الرقيق – كما يرينه – مفسِّرات بأنَّ ما آل إليه حالنا إنما من قبيل "العاقبة الأخلاقية" لأننا مدلَّلات، وأُخريات يتوسلن دخول المرحاض بسرعة لأنهنّ مُصابات بمرض السُكري، يطرقن الباب بعصبية وألم، يكدنَ يخترقنه ويقبضن على حلق من خلفه، صارخات:

- متى ستخرجين؟!

لتردَّ إحداهن من خلف الباب:

- ها أنا أعتصر أحشائي. هل ألفظها؟ اصبرنَ قليلاً! تبّاً لمن سمّاه بيت الخلاءَ!

دوّرتُ بصري في المكان، فلمحتُ امرأةً ذات وجه شاحب، ابتسمت لي، فرددتُ عليها بابتسامة. لكن، سرعان ما استعاد وجهي صرامته، كما لو أنَّ عضلات وجهي شتمتني لجعلها تتمغَّط عنوةً كي أبتسم للمرأة، وصوت في داخلي يهمس لي بدناءة: علامَ تبتسمان؟

صدر صوتٌ جامح من داخل المرحاض الآخر:

- يا إلهي! إحداهن تنتف شعر جسمها، ما الذي تفعلينه هنا يا عاهرة؟ إنه مرحاض! مرحاض!

ارتفع صوت آخر:

- اخفضي صوتك يا امرأة واسرعي! الطفلة تبكي.

وقفت طفلتان بشعر أشعث، وترويلٍ لا تزال آثاره على وجهيهما، عيونهن نصف مغمضات. كانتا تبكيان لحاجتهما الشديدة لدخول المرحاض، قابضتين على عانتيهما، متراقصتين في الممرّ الرملي للمرحاض الذي كنّا نقف فيه متراصّات.

كنتُ أحاول أن أشُقَّ طريقي نحو صنبور المياه في نهاية الممر، وأتجاوز هذه المسرحية التراجيدية المُملة. ولسوء عاقبتي، عندما وصلتُ لم أجد ماءً في الصنبور. فتحتُ راحتي فوجدتها فارغة من سائل الجلي الأصفر الذي اشترته أمي بالأمس. لم أجد سوى آثار مُخاطه الدّبِق على كفّي اليُسرى وخيط متطاير على الرمال من ورائي. هل كان السائل يتساقط من يدي طوال الطريق؟ تساءلتُ.

حاولتُ أن أُدير مقبض الصنبور للخلف وللأمام، يحدوني أملٌ زائف في نزول خيط هزيل من الماء، لكن لم تنزل قطرةٌ واحدة.

جمعتُ جسدي المتهاوي، وقد اجتاحه غضبٌ وخيبةٌ ونقمةٌ وأسئلةٌ لا حصر لها. سارعتُ بتجاوز الممر الرملي المزدحم بالنسوة الغاضبات إلى الشارع. لم أستطِع أن أُواري دمعي، فبكيت.

بكيتُ بكل كياني وروحي.

لعنتُ العالم، والبشر والحضارة والإنسانية.

لعنتُ نفسي والاحتلال وغزة وبحرها الذي أُحبُّه حبّاً مُتعباً ووحيداً، كما أحببتُ دائماً كلَّ ما في هذه البقعة من الأرض.

أجهشتُ بالبكاء طوال الطريق. لم أخجل من المارة، ولا من البيوت، ولا من الأرض التي أمشي فوقها.

أمطرتُ الأرضَ ببكائي في الذهاب والإياب، لكنها لم تكن ترتوي أبداً، سواء سالَ عليها ماء أو دم. اعتُصرتْ عيناي من شدَّة النحيب.

وصلتُ إلى الخيمة وارتميتُ على الأرض، كمحاربٍ تداعى على ركبتيه في ساحة معركة، بعد أن مزقّته السيوف، فسُفحت دماؤه وآماله.

ضجّت أسئلةٌ كثيرة في رأسي.

هل يمكن أن يكون الوطن منفى؟

هل هناك منفى في المنفى؟

ما البيت؟

هل البيت هو الوطن؟ أم الوطن كلُّه بيت؟

إذا كان الوطن هو البيت، لماذا أشعر بالاغتراب في رفح التي لا تبعُد عن خان يونس، مدينتي، سوى عشر دقائق؟

ولماذا خفتُ من شعوري حين تخيَّلتُ نفسي في ردهة بيتنا عندما طهت أمي ملوخية ومقلوبة بعد ستة أشهر من الانقطاع، مع أنني لستُ في البيت، بيتنا؟

يومها، قلتُ بصوت مرتفع: "أهذا ما يريده الاحتلال حقاً؟ أن أشعرَ بالبيت في ما يُذكِّر به؟!"

كيف أشعر أنني في بيتي وأنا لستُ فيه؟

كيف أكون خارج وطني وأنا فيه؟

نظرتُ إلى يدي فوجدتُها جافة من صقيع يناير، فيما تحول الصابون السائل الأصفر إلى مسحوق أبيض متجمِّد بين أصابعي.

غرفتي

سجا اللحام

المدينة حزينة. كلُّ شيء فيها حزين؛ السماء التي ترتجف تحت وطأة رعب المسيّرات الإسرائيلية، والشمس المختبئة بين الغيوم الكثيفة، والهواء المترقِّب بوجل. صوت القصف المتواصل والمخيف كان يزيد من سرعة نبضات قلبي. لم تكن الدبابات الإسرائيلية تبعد عن بيتنا سوى بضعة أمتار.

ماذا بعد؟ ماذا سيحلُّ بنا؟ إلى أين سنذهب؟ أسئلة كثيرة كانت تتصادم في رأسي.

كان الخوف يسيطر على المدينة، و"النزوح" هي الكلمة التي تتردد على لسان كل أب خائف على عائلته؛ أبي منهم.

جهَّزتُ أنا وأمي حقيبة لكلٍّ واحد من إخوتي، وضعنا فيها بعض الملابس التي تقيهم من برد الشتاء القارس، وأوراقهم الرسمية. وحين انتهيتُ من حقائبهم، بدأتُ بتجهيز حقيبتي. كان قلبي يحمل الكثير من القهر والأوجاع. وقفتُ أمام خزانتي الممتلئة بالملابس الجميلة وباهظة الثمن، أعاينها بصمت.

"ماذا آخذ؟ وماذا أترك؟"

أنا الابنة الكبرى لعائلتي، وأيضاً البنت الوحيدة المُدلَّلة بين خمسة صبيان. لم يكن أبي يبخل علينا بأي شيء، من ملابس أو هدايا، وأي شيء كنّا نريده.

"كيف سأرحل عن البيت، وأترك كل تلك الأشياء الغالية على قلبي؟"

عيناي مسحتا مكتبي الكائن تحت النافذة التي تُطل على بيوت جيراننا. كان يضمُّ دفاتري وكتبي الجامعية وأقلامي الملونة بجميع أشكالها؛ أوراق مُلصقة على سطح

المكتب تحمل عباراتٍ تحفيزيةً أُردِّدها لنفسي، وقد أُدندنها كأغنية لحنها يُعزف في قلبي.

"هنا صدَّقتُ حلمي وبدأت".

"قوم، قوم وعدّي الصعب، قوم، يوم هتضحكلك، ويوم تمشي عكس معاك، وعادي م الحياة دي يوم، ويوم فضي قلبك من الهموم، اكسب الدنيا دي قوم".

كنتُ قد رتَّبتُ مكتبي بعناية. تأملتُ كتبي التي كان يتعين عليَّ أن أودِّعها. لا أعرف ما إذا كانت ستنجو من الإبادة التي تسحق لحمنا وروحنا. حلمي كان أن أتخرج من الجامعة وأعمل معلِّمة. كان هذا حلم عائلتي أيضاً. لكن الحلم تهاوى مع ما تبقى من أحلامي تحت أشلاء البيوت. جيش الاحتلال أخرجنا من بيوتنا قسراً. "يا له من صهيوني لَعين!"، بكيتُ بحرقة فيما كنتُ أتمتمُ بغضب.

مسحتُ عن كتبي الغبار المتراكم بسبب القصف المُجاور لبيتنا، كما لو كنتُ أمسح وجه طفل بحنان أم، وخبَّأتُها في خزانتي.

بعد أن انتهيتُ من تحضير حقيبتي، ألقيتُ نظرةَ وداع على غُرفتي بالذكريات الكثيرة الموزَّعة فيها. مرَّ شريط حياتي، التي بدت لي قصيرة جداً، أمام عيني فبكيتُ مرة أُخرى.

عزَّ عليَّ فِراقُ بيتي. عزَّ عليَّ فراق غرفتي، مأمني الوحيد، وملاذي، وبيتي الشخصي في البيت. أغلقتُ باب الغرفة كالمُعتاد على أمل أن أعودَ لها يوماً، وتعود الأيام، وتعود الحياة، وتعود أحلامي التي تنتظرني.

كل دقيقة حياة

رزق أحمد

في هذا الزمن المجرَّد من العواطف، حيث العدوان بلا نهاية ونزيف الموت لا ينقطع، غدت المودة والدفء بين الأسر النازحة من قبيل الترف. وإذ يغرق الجميع في وحْل الصراع اليومي من أجل البقاء، نستمرُّ في التنقُّل من مكان إلى آخر، فقط للإبقاء على حياة لم تعُد تشبه أي شيء له علاقة بالحياة.

بدأت ألوان الأماكن تتلاشى وتذوب في الركام الرمادي الباهت، فيما كانت بهجة ماضينا القريب تتسرَّبُ من بين أصابعنا، وذكريات الأمس تسقط من ثقوب الروح التي اهترأت. تركنا وراءنا بيتاً كبيراً، قلبُه أكبر؛ احتوى حكاياتنا، وأحلامنا، وأفراحنا، وأوجاعنا.

أذكر ذلك كما لو كان من حياةٍ أخرى، مستلقياً على سريري، تملأ نفحات عطر جوز الهند الجو، أخطِّط نهاري في مفكِّرتي، وأدوِّن تفاصيل حياتي؛ ما كان منها عادياً وعابراً، وما كان ذا معنى – لي أنا على الأقل. ثم كأن الحياة انتقلت فجأة إلى فصل كابوسي، فبعد مكالمة قصيرة من جيش الاحتلال الإسرائيلي لم تتجاوز الثواني، أُجبرنا على الرحيل من بيتنا الواسع، بغرفه الأنيقة ولمسات أمي الرقيقة. وجدنا أنفسنا في كوخ من النايلون، جزء منه شفاف، بالكاد يسترنا، والجزء الآخر أسود يحبسُنا في حرٍّ خانق. بنينا الكوخ من أقمشة بالية، من فساتين جدّتي الراحلة، ومن بطانيات أطفال حملت رسوم شخصيات الأبطال الخارقين الذين كانوا يُزيِّنون غرف طفولتنا منذ زمن بعيد.

لم ينتهِ الأمر عند ذلك. فهذا الكوخ، الذي تقاسمته أربع عائلات، تحوّل إلى مأوى مؤقت، نحمله معنا، من "منطقة آمنة" مزعومة إلى أخرى. أطلقنا عليه اسم "الرياح الأربع"، ثم لاحقاً "الكوبونات الأربع"، في إشارة إلى قسائم المساعدات الغذائية الأربع التي تمنحها لنا المؤسسات الإغاثية، حيث كانت ألوانها تتبدَّل

مع كل تجديد، فيما نحن كما نحن، عالقون في البؤس والحاجة والانتظار العبثي إلى ما لا نهاية.

كان اتخاذ القرار بالنزوح من منطقة إلى أخرى فعلاً جماعياً، يتركز فيه النقاش في كل مرة على سؤالين: متى نرحل؟ وإلى أين نرحل؟ بينما نحاول في الأثناء استقصاء السُّبل لتفادي قصف الجيش الإسرائيلي بكل ما أوتينا من حذر، والقليل من الحظ. ففي جميع الأحوال، لم نكن نعرف أين يمكن أن يقع القصف، ومتى، وكيف. كانت الطاولة الخشبية الصغيرة المتهالكة في الكوخ تتحوّل إلى غرفة عمليات طارئة، نجتمع حولها على نبضٍ واحد؛ الجدّ، والآباء، والإخوة، والأبناء والبنات، والأحفاد، نتشاور في قرارات مصيرية.

في أغلب الأحيان، كانت صباحاتنا المبكرة أكثر من المعتاد تبدأ بنداءات الباعة الذين تشقُّ أصواتهم السماء الملغَّمة بـ "الزنّانات"، يبيعون في المخيم الحليب والخبز. كنا نتقاسم طعامنا القليل، وكان الجميع يتشاركون مهام الطبخ والتنظيف اليومي. وفي الليل، كنا نضحك ونحن نرتِّب فراشنا على الأرض، نكدّس أجسادنا في المساحة الضيقة لنسرق بضع ساعات من النوم.

لا توجد مرآة في الكوخ. وإذا رغب أحدنا في ترتيب مظهره الخارجي، فإنه يلجأ إلى أمي حنان، الملكة الرقيقة التي تملأ قلوبنا حناناً، والمرآة التي ترانا جميلين ووسيمين كيفما كنا. أستعرض هيئتي أمام أختي هالة، التي تكبرني، فتضحك على شكلي بالبنطلون الذي بالكاد يثبت على خصري، وقد اضطررتُ إلى لفِّ الحزام حوله مرة ونصف المرة. وعندما أهمُّ بالخروج، ينبِّه عليَّ أخي آدم قائلاً:

- لا تتأخر في الخارج! أريد أن أرتدي البنطلون عندما أخرج لاحقاً.

عند عودتي إلى الكوخ أتأمل وجوه الأحفاد – أبناء وبنات إخوتي – وقد سفعت شمسُ الصيف بشرتهم، يلبسون ثياباً لا تميز بين الصبي والبنت، مسدِّدين نظرات يملؤها التعب والجوع وصبر طويل على شُحّ المساعدات في مخيمنا.

أسأل هنادي:

- شو غدا اليوم؟

تمنحني ابتسامةً خفيفة، وتجيب فيما تُقلِّب الطعام في القدر على النار:

- فاصوليا . . . بس بدنا نعمل رز للصغار بعدد المعالق . . . والكبار ياكلوا الفاصوليا بالخبز.

كانت هنادي قد حلَّت محلّ أمي، كي تخفِّف عنها عناء الطهي بالقرب من النار في هذا الحرّ اللاهب. قالت لتحمّسنا أكثر:

- راح أحضّر سلطة، لكن بدون طحينة لأنها غالية.

والحق أنَّ هنادي لها "نَفَس" في الطبخ، فهي تطهو بحب، والسلطة التي تعدُّها لا يُعلى عليها.

واقعنا اليوم لا يتعدّى متراً مربّعاً واحداً، بالكاد يتّسع لجلوسنا معاً. رائحةُ البصل ومرق المكعَّبات، بديلاً عن اللحم، تملأ الأجواء، بينما يمسح أحدُنا الطاولة بحذر، متفادياً مساميرها المنتشرة على سطحها بعشوائية؛ بعضها كما لو كانت قد نبتت كأشواك حادة. ينادي والدي علينا لتناول الطعام. حتى في نزوحنا، فإن لمَّة العائلة على المائدة، سواء أكانت حول طاولة متهالكة أو حصيرة مهترئة على الأرض، شيء مقدَّس. كان والدي قد أعدَّ طبقاً مُحبَّباً، من البصل المفروم والتوابل، تزيِّنُه خلطةٌ من أوراق الريحان المفرومة والفلفل الأخضر الحار والثوم، في تشكيل لوني شهي وجذاب.

"هناك حديث عن هدنة"، ينقل لنا شقيقي الأكبر هشام الأخبار "الحلوة" بنبرة عكست تفاؤلاً مبالغاً به. يرُد والدي، والكرسي المتهالك يئنُّ تحت جسده، وهو يزيِّن الطعام بالتتبيلة الحارة، تحاصرُه نار الموقد في حرّ الصيف:

- الله كبير. أهم شيء أنكم بخير، وكل شيء آخر يهون.

نُحضِر ما تيسَّر من الفاكهة، ونضعها على المائدة، فيوجِّه لنا أبي تعليماته:

- كلوا باعتدال، عشان الخبز يكفي الجميع، والكل يشبع ومحدّش يقول: جوعان.

وبالطبع، يتعين غسل المواعين، وتلميعها، كقاعدة حملناها من بيتنا في حقبة ما قبل النزوح. ثم تتحوّل مائدة الطعام إلى مائدة مستديرة للنقاش السياسي،

نتبادل حولها الآراء والتحليلات بشأن مجريات العدوان، كما لو كنا في بثٍّ حيّ لبرنامج "الاتجاه المعاكس". تضحك أمّي وتقول: "خلّونا نركز على حالنا ووضعنا"، ثم تتنهّد، مذكّرةً إيّانا كيف كنّا نعيش في بحبوحة، وكيف أصبحنا اليوم نعتمد على التكيّات.

والغريب أنّ وجودنا معاً في هذه الأوقات المستحيلة صار أجمل. ألفة جديدة نشأت بيننا، لا عتاب فيها ولا تذمُّر ولا ندم، ربما لأن كل دقيقة حياة تعني حياة حقيقية، لا يمكن التعامل معها كأمر مسلَّم به.

في العصر، نجتمعُ مع أبي وأمي وجدّي في فناء رملي تزيّنه شتلات من الريحان التي جلبناها معنا من بيتنا، كتذكار لما نحن عليه، وإلى أين ننتمي. نتبادلُ الحديث عن شجرة العائلة، نعدِّدُ أسماء من استشهدوا، ونحصي الجرحى، اسماً وعُمراً وقصةً، ونستذكرُ الأصل الطيب، نستعيدُ قصصَهم ومواقفَهم وحياتهم الغنية، التي أغنتنا، فيما يُنصتُ الأحفاد بكل حواسهم، قبل أن يمطرونا بكل أنواع الأسئلة. "سيِدي! كيف حبّيت سِتّي وهي المصريّة القويّة، وأنتَ "غلبان" معها؟"، يضحكون وهم يسألون، فيعيد جدّي سرد الحكاية التي سمعوها مراراً، كأنها تُروى للمرة الأولى.

حلوى المساء المتاحة بسكويت من المعونات الغذائية، نأكله مع شاي نعدُّه على الحطب؛ على نار تشتعل حيناً وتنطفئ حيناً آخر. تنسابُ دموع أبي بصمت، فتمسحُ عن وجهه سواد النار. تنفرج عن شفتيه ابتسامة، كأنه يطمئننا أننا سنكون بخير، ويسأل: "من سيجلب الحطب غداً؟"، فلا يجيبه أحد. بل ننهض جميعاً، نهرب إلى النوم، قبل أن يُكلِّف أيّاً منا بالمهمة، ونغفو قبل أن تستيقظ صراصير الليل.

ويبدأ صباحٌ جديد، وحياةٌ جديدة. توقظنا خشخشةٌ خفيفة من راديو قديم، سلكُه ممتدّ من عمود الكوخ إلى معصم أبي. أما الخبر الجميل هذا اليوم، فهو انخفاض سعر البيض، فثماني بيضات الآن أصبحت بعشرة شواكل.

اليوم، أعلنت أمي أن الغداء "شكشوكة". الجميع يحب الشكشوكة ما عداي، فكنتُ أنتقي البيض والفلفل الأخضر، وأترك البندورة. لكن الجوع غيّرَ كلَّ شيء، إذ أتناولها حالياً بشهية. عائلتي اعتادت منذ زمن على انتقائيتي المزعجة في الأكل. وكانت أمي، في الماضي، تُعدُّ أطباقاً مختلفة لترضي أذواقنا المختلفة. أما الآن، فنأكل جميعاً كلَّ شيء وأيَّ شيء، ومن نفس الصحن، وبغبطة مقترنة بالرضا.

في الليل، يكون فراشنا مشتركاً أيضاً. ينام أبي وأمي على مرتبة، وتنام آية، دلوعتنا وأصغر بنات العائلة، على مرتبة، فيما نتمدَّد، نحن البقية، جنباً إلى جنب فوق بطانيات شتوية ثقيلة تختزن الحرارة. ومع ذلك، نتدبَّر أمرنا ونحتمل الوضع الصعب، شاعرين بالدفء والاطمئنان، وبأن وجودنا معاً يقلِّل إحساسَنا بالخطر، وقد يبعده عنّا تماماً.

يبقى والدي مستيقظاً طوال الليل، يسهر علينا. لا ينام إلا في النهار، وهي عادةٌ اكتسبها منذ نزوحنا الأوّل إلى رفح، إذ لم يطاوعه قلبه أن يغفو بينما عائلته عرضة لخطر الموت في الليل. أتساءل أحياناً إن كنتُ سأكون أباً صالحاً مثله يوماً ما.

مع الأيام، لا نملك إلا أن نضحك على مفارقة أخرى من مفارقات حياة الخيم: الملابس المشتركة؛ فقد فقدنا جميعاً الكثير من الوزن، حتى أصبحنا الآن في المقاسُ نفسه تقريباً، وصارت ملابسنا القليلة تناسب الجميع، لم يعد أحد يزداد وزناً، لكن الحب ازداد، صار أكبر وأعمق.

وسيأتي الغد، وتتكرّر الأشياء ذاتها، و"ترجع حليمة لعادتها القديمة"، كما يقول المثل.

ستوزع أمي علينا مهامنا: من يجلب الماء؟ من يقف في طابور الخبز؟ من يجمع الحطب؟

القرار

خديجة أبو لبدة

ليلةٌ أخرى من ليالي الشتاء الذي لا يفرق بين بيت أو خيمة. أزيز الطائرات المسيّرة كالطنين، لا ينفك يضرب رأسي. أفكاري تتشابك مع السرير، وقد بُعثرت فوقه بفوضوية. أذناي تلتقطان أصوات القذائف والمدافع وهدير البحر. عيناي تتبَعان قصاصات الملاحظات الملتصقة على ظهر السرير الذي انتفخت أليافه الخشبية إثر رطوبة البيت الأسبستي. كان سقفنا قد تشقَّق بفعل الشظايا التي هرَّت فوقه حين قُصف بيت جارنا الأسمنتي. ظل سقف بيتنا الأسبستي صامداً، إلا أنه لم يخلُ من الانكسارات والشروخ التي تفاقمت داخله، والتي تجعل خيالك الخصب يرى فيها أشكالاً عدَّة.

عيناي تسرقان الخربشات والخطوط المتشابكة التي رسمها أخي قاسم على ظهر السرير. يُدهشك ما يمكن لِيدٍ وقلمٍ وحيد أن تبوحا به من مشاعر الفنان وأفكاره عبر تشكيلات غير مفهومة. لم تفلح لطخة اللون البنفسجي التي أضفتُها في طمس التشكيلات، إذ شكّلت طبقةً لونيةً شفافة فوقها، أشبه بغلالة ليليكة شاحبة، جعلت الرسمة أكثر سوريالية. لايزال تذمُّر قاسم وصراخه لأنني أفسدتُ فنَّه يتردَّدُ في أذني كلما نظرتُ إليها. ابتسمتُ تعجُّباً. لم أكن أجيدُ شيئاً إلا المشاكسة. ولم أكن أعلم بأن الخطوط المتشابكة والمنحنيات المتداخلة على هيئة حصان، يبدو أنه يطير وخصلات شعره للوراء وذيله يحاول اللحاق به، نوع من أنواع الفن.

كنتُ شقيّةً عندما كان الأمر يتعلق بالسرير، فقد كان الحصول على سرير في ذلك الوقت كالحصول على جائزة نوبل. ومن غيظي لأنني لم أكن أمتلك واحداً مثله، كنتُ أستولي عليه في النهار. وكانت تشتعل حربٌ بيني وبين قاسم، تنتهي في كل مرة بتوبيخ أمي لي.

كانت آثار يديّ الملطختين باللون البنفسجي، كمحاولة عقيمة لإثبات ملكيتي، قد صاغت أشكالاً عجيبة على أرجُل السرير. فاحت من السرير رائحة عطنة. بدت قوائمه الغليظة، كأنها واقفة بصعوبة، كرجل شاخ في الحرب فجأة، فكان على وشك أن يتداعى. ترنَّخت الرائحة أكثر مع المطر المتسلِّل إلى البيت عبر حوائطه التي كانت لا تزال منتصبةً بشيء من الكبرياء، وقد نجت حتى اللحظة من القصف.

جلستُ متربِّعةً على السرير، رأسي يتقلُّب بين أفكاري، أحاول أن أترجم خربشات قاسم إلى كلمات على دفتر صغير. سقط القلم من يدي على صوت شقيقي الأكبر أحمد، الذي بادرني بوجه بشوش، وإن طوى خبراً كان واثقاً بأنني لن أكون سعيدة به:

- غادة، أختي الحبيبة، أعلم جيداً ما يعنيه هذا السرير لك، كيف لا وقد شاهدتُ مدى تعلقك به بعد موت قاسم.

حين بدأ أحمد بهذه المقدمة فهمتُ على الفور ماذا سيحدث بعدها؛ لا بدَّ وأن أسطوانة الغاز لن تصل قريباً، وبما أننا كنّا قد حرقنا كل شيء نملكه، كوقود، فعلى الأرجح أنه سيطلب مني أن يأخذ السرير. يا إلهي! لا تجعله يطلب مني ذلك. لن أتمكن من الاعتراض في هذا الوضع الميؤوس منه. ارتجفت شفتاي بشهقة خافتة.

تابع قائلاً:

- ما زلتُ أذكر ما حدث كأنه وقع أمس، حين كنتِ تنادين على قاسم، وهو مسجى على السرير، ممسكةً بيده، تحاولين الإبقاء على حياته، قبل أن يلفظ آخر أنفاسه. أعلم كيف ظللتِ مقيمةً فوق هذا السرير في فترة العزاء، وكيف رفضتِ بيعه لأيٍّ كان، لكن الأمر فاق حيلتي يا أختي. هذا الألم افترسنا، ومن يعلم مدى الألم مثلنا نحن الذين فقدنا في مواسم القتل الجماعي أماً وأباً، وخرجنا منها بأخ التهمه المرض بعدها.

سكت أحمد قليلاً وهو ينظر إلى عيني بانكسار وترجٍّ. "لا بد أنه سيطلبه"، حدَّثتُ نفسي، "أرجوك يا أخي، اقرأ عيني جيداً! لا أستطيع أن أتخلى عنه، لا تكمل حديثك"، صحتُ في جوفي، لكنه واصل:

- أنت تعلمين مثلي حجم المسؤولية علينا، بالكاد أستطيع توفير الطعام، لم نعد نملك شيئاً يصلح للوقود إلا هذا السرير.

- كيف سأتخلى عنه؟ ألا توجد طريقة أخرى؟

- أنتِ تعلمين جيداً أنني لم أكن لأطلب منكِ التخلي عنه لو كان لدي خيار آخر.

انعقد حاجباه الدقيقان، غصَّت نبرة صوته بالاختناق، وأطلق تنهيدةً عالية، وقال بألم:

- فاق الوضع قدرتي على التحمُّل. هل أحرق نفسي؟ لقد تعبتُ يا أختي. افهميني رجاءً! تفهَّمي انكساري لأنّني أطلب منك هذا الطلب!

ظللتُ صامتة، لا أعرف ماذا أجيبه. كنتُ أعي وضعنا جيداً، لكن عزَّ عليَّ التخلي عن قاسم. السرير كان آخر آثارنا معاً. نظرتُ إلى أحمد واجمة. لم أجد كلمات تعبِّر عن الفراغ الذي بدأ يسحبني عميقاً، فيما كان خشب السرير يئنّ، وجدران البيت الهزيلة تميل فوقي. لابد أن صمتي عبَّر له عمّا بداخلي، إذ قال بنبرة متوسِّلة:

- لن أضغط عليكِ أكثر إذا كنتِ غير راغبة في التخلي عن السرير، لكن فكِّري قليلاً، هل ذكرى أحبابنا الراحلين أهم من أحبابنا الأحياء؟

توغّلت كلماته في داخلي. ظلَّ الصمتُ يلتهم مشاعري، قبل أن تتمرَّدَ أخيراً، لأدفع نفسي بقوة خارج الفراغ قبل أن أبلغ قاعَه. كيف يطلب مني أحمد أن أتخلى عن السرير؟! أعلم أن الواقع قاسٍ، لكن القرار أقسى. لماذا يجب أن نتخلى عن أشيائنا؟ أمن أجل حياة قد لا تُكتَب لنا؟ لماذا لا أكون أنانيةً في مشاعري؟ ظللتُ أصرخ بصمت، وأرمي جميع الأشياء التي تصلح للكسر، بما في ذلك خاطري. تمرَّغ جسدي في السرير بصمتٍ أثقله ضجيج أفكاري.

امتدَّت يدي إلى القلم الملقى بجوار رِجل السرير. لم يكن السرير مصنوعاً من خشب الزان أو البلوط، لكنه خشب قديم يحمل ذكريات غالية جداً. كتبتُ بعض الملاحظات على قصاصات وألصقتُها على ظهر السرير.

"هل ذكرى أحبابنا الراحلين أهم من أحبابنا الأحياء؟"

"هل هناك طريقة للحصول على المال أثناء الإبادة دون أن نقتل شيئاً فينا؟"

"أن يموت المرء على فراش المرض رفاهية. على الأقل هناك فراش".

"النار لن تأتي على الخشب فقط. أسمع صوت النار. ها أنا أسمع صوت طقطقة جسدي".

استمرت أفكاري المبعثرة ترفس الأغطية إلى أن انبلج الفجر. بدأت بجمع الشراشف والأغطية من السرير. تأمَّلتُه، وحفظتُ تفاصيله الدقيقة والمؤلمة، وقد أصاب عينيّ الغمام.

قرأتُ القصاصات المثبَّتة عليه كإرثي الشخصي. ثم جلستُ أمام النار التي كانت تلتهم خربشات قاسم وتشكيلاته، في حالة عزاء متجدِّد، أرتدي كنزةً سوداء، وأراقبُ الدخان الرمادي الذي يصعد إلى السماء. كانت النسائم الرقيقة تواسيني بطريقتها المعهودة، تحمل معها الدخان الذي يضمُّني بدفء. رائحة الخشب كانت غير مألوفة. أغمضتُ عينيَّ لأركز أكثر. تخيَّلتُ النيران تعبقُ برائحة قاسم. عشتُ لبرهة في عالم مخادع جميل، كأنني بين ذراعيه أشتم رائحته، وأستند إلى صدره الدافئ. فتحتُ عينيَّ المليئتين بالشوق لرؤيته. مددتُ يدي لألمسه، وقد سحرتني النارُ بلهيبها الذي أضاء وجهه. لكن النار ما لبثت أن انتفضت، لتدفع سحب الدخان نحوي بقوة. شعرتُ بالاختناق. تراجعتُ فيما كنتُ أسعل. كانت معمعة النيران التي علت فجأة كأنها تضحك من السراب الذي احتواني. تصاعد الدخان مرة أخرى، موشَّحاً بالسواد. سحبتُ يدي ببطء، أمسِّد صدري بأصابعي، عساي أبدِّد الذهول الذي تلبَّسني. ابتسمت شفتاي بتلقائية حين خُيِّلت إليَّ ضحكات قاسم مع صوت طقطقة الخشب المحترق. تُرى، أكان السرير سجناً له حبسته فيه أم سجناً لي؟

كانت القصاصات المثبتة على السرير تلامسها النار صعوداً؛ تأتي على كلماتها حرفاً، حرفاً، بدءاً من اللهب الأزرق المتَّقد، فالبرتقالي المتوهِّج، في مزيج لوني من ضياء النار.

جزءٌ من قصاصة أفلتت من اللهب المستعر. ظلَّت تتهادى في الهواء بخفَّة، قبل أن تحطَّ في حِجري. كان عليها كلمة واحدة لم تأتِ عليها النار: "الأحياء".

هذيان

عمرو النجار

في كل مساء، إما الصمت المتوتر أو الصوت المدوّي داخل رأسك، كلاهما يجتاحان عقلكَ؛ عقلكَ الذي لم يعُد قادراً على التفكير أو التصوُّر أو حتى تقبُّل أي شيء. يبدأ قلبُكَ ينبضُ بسرعة، تقبضُ عليك مشاعر فقدان الحرية، وفقدان الأمل، وفقدان الشغف، وفقدان الحنان، وفقدان الأمان. حتى دخول الحمام المزعج، المعتم، الضيق، بالرائحة الكريهة النتنة، يتحول إلى مصدر رعب.

هناك شيء ثقيلٌ يربضُ فوق ظهري، لا أقدر على وصف الألم. تائهٌ أنا، أتحدَّثُ مع نفسي، مصدوم من هول المشاعر والأفكار المضطرمة في داخلي. أريدُ أن أكتبَ عن كل شيء، وأتحدَّث عن كل شيء، لكنني لا أعرف بماذا أبدأ. عن ماذا أكتب؟ عن هذه النكبة الثانية؟ أم الثالثة؟ لم أعُد أعرف. هل يمكن حقاً أن يكون بعد هذه الإبادة مستقبل؟ هل ستكون هناك حياة بعدها؟ هل هناك موتٌ أكثر من الموت الجاثم فوقنا؟

الأشياء الجميلة كانت قبل هذا كله، الحنين إلى بيتنا الذي شُيِّد حديثاً، بيت أبي بتفاصيله المعمارية الجميلة التي عكست اهتمامه بأدق الأمور؛ صوت أمي القريب والبعيد، الحاضر في كل زاوية من زوايا البيت؛ أبي عند عودته إلى البيت وما كان يجلبه معه من جلَبَة منعشة؛ صوت الباب حين كان يفتحه، خطواته عند الدخول، صوت حذائه المُلمَّع دوماً فوق البلاطات النظيفة؛ إخوتي أحدهم يشجِّع فريقه الكروي المفضل؛ أختي في غرفتها، تتفنَّنُ في تحديد عينيها بالكحل لإبراز اتساعهما، ووضع كريمات ذات ألوان ترابية على بشرتها، فيما تضيء أشعة الشمس، التي تتخلَّل زوايا البيت، عينيها العسليتين فتزهر الحياة من حولها.

كانت الورود في الأصص والأحواض تملأ البيت بأريجها. وكانت النسائم تحرك روحي فيما ترفرف الستائر مع كل هبّة هواء رقيقة. كنتُ أرفع صوت الراديو على أغنية

"أمل حياتي" لأم كلثوم، أطربُ لها مع رشفات القهوة التي يتضوَّعُ فضاء المنزل بها، تُشعرني بأنَّ كلَّ شيء في العالم على ما يرام، وأنَّ كل شيء كما يجب أن يكون عليه. كانت الأصداف والحصى تزيِّنُ جنبات الحديقة. الأريكة القديمة في الحديقة التي أتت الرياح وتقلُّبات الشمس على خشبها ظلت متينةً وصامدة. من حولها، همست أشجار النخيل بحضورها الطاغي. كل شيء كان يحضنني، حتى أضنَتْني ذكرى الحب.

نعم، بيتُنا كان وطناً كبيراً، وإن شُيِّد على بقعة أرض لا تتجاوز دونمين، ورثناها من جدّي. لم يكن بيتُنا يشبه هذا المكان الذي نعيش فيه الآن. كثيراً ما كنتُ أجلس أتأمَّله، متسائلاً بيني وبين نفسي: كيف لهذا "المسكن"، كحيز صغير في عالم كبير، أن يجعلك دوماً في علاقة حب كبيرة ومتجدِّدة معه باستمرار؟ كان هناك تناغم جميل بين حجارته وألوانه وأثاثه وتصميمه، يخاطب القلب.

كيف لشيء حديث البناء قادرٌ على احتضان عمّي الذي عاد بعد غياب خمسة وأربعين عاماً في الغربة، ليكون هذا مستقرّه الأخير في الدنيا؟ لم يشأ عمّي أبداً مغادرة البيت أو فنائه، فقد وجد فيه كل ما يريده.

كنتُ دائماً مزهواً بالبيت، بيتنا الذي كان يتَّسع للعالم وبشر العالم. احتضن مناسباتنا العائلية، وحكاياتنا، وحفلات خطوبة أبناء العمومة، واستقبال المغتربين وتوديع المسافرين، وولائم مع الأقارب والصحب، ونقاشات ساخنة وجدالات عقيمة، وسهرات السمر والأنس.

آخ من وجع الروح! لا أستطيع مواصلة الكتابة، مع أن عقلي مزدحم بالأفكار والذكريات. أشعر بأنني مشتَّت، مبعثر، ضعيف.

تمرُّ أمام عيني ومضات من ذكرياتي عندما كنّا نذهبُ لزيارة عمّاتي، من باب "صلة الرحم"، ليُضفنَ إلى حياتنا دفئاً مضاعفاً. هذه الزيارات انقطعت إلى الأبد. شقيقات أبي وعددٌ من أبنائهن وأحفادهن رحلوا في غمضة عين تحت الركام. لم نكن هناك لنحتضنهم في لحظاتهم الأخيرة. يا ترى، بماذا كانوا يفكرون؟ هل كانوا يشعرون بالموت يدنو منهم؟ هل كانوا خائفين؟ هل استشهدوا جميعهم في آنٍ واحد؟ هل لوَّح أحدهم بيده طلباً للنجاة لكن لا مجيب؟

زوج خالتي المرح وابنتاه سلمى وليلى انهار عليهم منزلٌ من تسعة طوابق. ارتقت أرواحُهم لمعانقة الملائكة. لكن، كيف تحمَّلوا موتاً كهذا؟ أنا متيقِّن أنهم لم

يموتوا على الفور. هل رأوا موتهم يحدِّق بهم؟ هل شاهدوه يقبض عليهم؟ رائحتهم كانت جميلة دائماً. هل تغيرت هذه الرائحة العطرة عندما اختلطت بالتراب والبارود والدم؟ هل ستصبح زكيَّة مع استشهادهم؟ أم قد يتعيَّن عليك ارتداء كمّامة كي تصدَّ عنك رائحة تحلُّل أجسادهم؟ كيف سيكونون عندما يخرج الدود منهم؟

سلمى وليلى كانتا تنتظران طرف خيط تقبضان عليه ليتمَّ انتشالهما من تحت الأنقاض. لم تعرفا إلا الفن والموسيقى. أناملهما كانت صديقةً للنغم وريشة الألوان، عبرهما أرسلتا رسائل حبٍّ إلى أولئك ممَّن عرفوهما. أتخيَّلهما تبكيان، تريدان أمهما، أو أي أحد يخفِّف من روعهما.

أريد أن أبكي، لكن لا وقت للبكاء.

أذكر حديقة بيتنا، التي كانت فيما مضى تعجُّ بأصوات ضحكات أبناء عمومتي ونكاتهم. لقد ذهبوا. لماذا ذهبوا وتركوني وحدي أواجه هذا الصمت الهائل؟

في بالي أصدقائي الذين كانوا يتباهون بإنجازاتهم، أحلامهم كانت تلامس السماء. كانوا يحبّون التجمُّع في حديقتنا التي شكلت مساحةً رحبةً لموسيقاهم وأغنياتهم، وتساؤلاتهم الوجودية الكبرى. أتذكَّر أحدهم يسأل آخر:

- تخيَّل لو استشهدنا!

ليجيبه:

- محلاها الشهادة! بس والله لسّا بدري! يعني لو نحقق أحلامنا، ونعمّر الأرض إلّي تعبنا عشانها، وبعدين يا أهلاً بالشهادة لو مكتوبة إلنا.

ويكمل:

- إحنا مش خايفين! بس ليس الآن!

لكنهم استشهدوا خائفين ومرتجفين. لن أنسى محادثتي الأخيرة معهم. كنتُ أشعر برجفة أصابعهم حين كانوا يراسلونني عبر الموبايل. كنتُ أكاد أسمع نبضات قلوبهم

الوجلة، وكنتُ أستشعر برودة أجسادهم المرتعشة. ذهبوا دون نظرة أخيرة منّي، أو حتى عناق أزيل عنهم من خلاله بعض الخوف الذي بداخلهم. أخذوا قلبي معهم.

كنّا قد تعاهدنا بأن نبقى معاً، وأن نتخطّى كل هذا سوياً. وعدوني، وأنا صدَّقتُ الوعد.

بينما كنتُ أكتب، ظهر القمر من بين الغيوم، يسكبُ بهاءه عبر النافذة. التمعت عيناي. ما أحلاه! في حلكة الليل، أنار القمر قلبي رغم حزني الشديد. كيف لشيء صغير وبعيد جداً، عابر كالسحر أو الوهم، أن يضيء أيامي المليئة بالسواد؟

الوضع هادئ نسبياً. الناس نيام. الجو بارد. والعقل غير مرتاح.

أسمع صوتاً ليس بعيداً. إنه جارنا أبو ياسر. كان يستمع إلى الراديو، ويتحدث مع نفسه قائلاً: "شكله فيه هدنة! أيوه! خلّي الواحد يتنفس شوية". سرَت في داخلي رعشة ترقُّب. جلستُ معتدلاً، مستعيراً فرحته. فجأة، انقطع صوت الراديو وصوت أبو ياسر. بعد لحظات سمعتُه يتمتم: "اخصْ! بطاريته خلصت"، وأطفأ كل شيء وتوجَّه للنوم، متذمِّراً، يلعن العالم.

نمتُ متأخراً، تسبقني دمعتي على الوسادة، واستيقظتُ باكراً. القهوة أقوى منبِّه بالنسبة لي، رائحتُها تحرِّكني. والدي يصنعها بعناية ولهفة، رغم أنَّ ثمنها أصبح باهظاً جداً، ولم يعد بمقدور أي شخص شراؤها. لكن أبي يعيش علاقة حب كبيرة مع قهوته، ولا يمكن أن يخونها. وأنا لا أستطيع أن أتجاهل نداءها كل صباح مهما كلَّفني ذلك.

يصنع أبي القهوة وهو يدندن بأغنية فيروز: "راجعين يا هوى راجعين، يا زهرة المساكين، راجعين يا هوى"، صوته يئنُّ بتوقه للرجوع إلى بيته. يُذكِّرني بالأيام الخوالي، قبل هذا كله. تُرى، هل سيرجع أبي يوماً إلى كينونة بيته؟ هل سنجتمع على طاولة سفرة واحدة نتبادل الحكايات وأخبار الناس مع وجبة عشاء خفيفة يصنعها هو، تحمل نفَسه الطيِّب؟

أستيقظُ أمام إغراء القهوة بهمَّة عالية. أرى أبي يبتسم وهو يناولني الفنجان، لتحتضنني رائحتها.

أصواتُ السيارات وعربات النقل تبدِّدُ سكون الصباح، وقد تداخلت معها لعلعة نداء بائعي مياه الشرب، وأصوات المارة الذين يطلقون الشتائم علناً – كما في دواخلهم، وصياح الأطفال الذين لا يعلمون بأي أرض سيعيشون أو يموتون. لكن لا بأس من قيامهم بصُنع طائرات ورقية بحماسة وإثارة كبيرتين، قد تلهيهم نوعاً ما عمّا هم فيه. شتّان ما بين هدوء القهوة وبين ضجيج الشارع.

هممتُ ببدء يوم جديد أخوض فيه معارك جديدة مع نفسي، ومع الناس، ومع الشوارع، ومع الشمس اللاهبة، للحصول على الطحين، ومياه الشرب، والطعام.

غادرتُ خيمتي أرتدي ملابسي الملعونة، التي تُذكِّرني كل يوم بهذه النكبة. سرتُ بخطوات ثقيلة وحزينة بين الناس وغبار السيارات والشمس الحارقة، أسألُ نفسي: كيف للأرض أن تحملَ كلَّ هذا الأسى؟ كل هذا القهر والحزن الساحق؟ كل هذا الثقل اللعين؟

أين الطريق؟ أنا تائه.

فاشينيستا

فاطمة عصفور

أجسادٌ ملقاةٌ على أرضية صفّ الحادي عشر في مدرسة مصطفى حافظ بمدينة خان يونس أنهكها التعب والخوف، يتوسطُّها جسد روزا، طويلة القامة، التي تفرد ذراعيها، مستيقظةً من نوم طويل، مرهِق، تخلّلته صور وأصوات شاحبة من الماضي. تتثاءب فيما تحاول أن تمدَّ ساقيها وذراعيها، فإذا بوجوه غريبة تحت قدميها، وأطفال مستلقين حول ذراعيها، ونساء تتزاحم أجسادهن، رؤوسهن مدفونة بالقرب من أقدامهن المتسخة – من قلة الماء – متكوّرات على أنفسهن، كي يتمكن الجميع من إيجاد حيّزٍ للنوم داخل الفصل، الذي لجأ فيه أكثر من مئة شخص، بين رُضَّع، وأطفال، وصبايا، ونساء، ومسنّات، ضمن خريطة متنوعة من المشاعر والسلوكيات والنزق والغضب المتلاطم.

معظم الوقت، لم تكن روزا تخلع غطاء الصلاة "التيفاني". نعالها، من علامة "غوتشي"، أصبح قطعةً مهترئةً يتناوب على ارتدائه جميع مَن في الفصل، مِن الأطفال والنساء، عند ذهابهم إلى الحمام الشبيه بمستنقع ذي رائحة نتنة، يقف على بابه خمسون شخصاً، على الأقل، ينتظرون دخول المرحاض الغاصّ بالفضلات لقضاء الحاجة، أو للاستحمام – وهو ما ندر – وسط عدم توفر الماء بشكل دائم، دون أن يعدم الأمر تبادل الصراخ والشتائم البذيئة على امتداد طابور الحمام.

في ظل هذه الأجواء، كان من الطبيعي أن ترتفع ضحكات بعض النساء، في زاوية الحمام، على نكتة فاحشة ترويها إحداهن هامسة، فيما يقضي بعض الأطفال وقت الانتظار الطويل في النطنطة واللهو حول أمّهاتهم، سريعات الغضب منهم ومن كل شيء.

كل يومين، تتعالى أصوات الصفير والزغاريد في مختلف أرجاء المدرسة لأن الماء أصبح متوفراً، وكأنهم وقعوا على كنز، فيبدأ الرجال والنساء والأطفال بجمع أوعيتهم للحصول على حصتهم.

كان لدى روزا قارورتان بحجم لترين، تملؤهما بالماء، عند توفره، للاستحمام وغسل بنطالها الجينز الذي نزحت به في بداية العدوان الإسرائيلي وبلوزتها البيضاء المكرمشة متعدِّدة الثنيات، وقد سلكت بهما سبلاً عرجاء. ظلت روزا مرتدية ملابسها نفسها لشهر كامل، تغسلها كل يومين وترتديها بمائها، ليتجمَّدَ جسدُها في برودة الشتاء.

فجأة، بدأت بالبكاء بصوت مرتفع دوّى في فضاء الصف، تقاطع مع صوت الصاروخ الذي سقط على أحد البيوت المجاورة، فكان صوت نحيبها أقوى من صوت الانفجار، وسط تلفُّت الجميع نحوها باندهاش، وهي تصرخ:

- هاي مو حياتي.. هاي مو أنا!

لم تفهم كيف لفاشينيستا ومصمِّمة أزياء ومبدعة مثلها أن تعيشَ هذا الواقع القذر. كانت يداها ترتجفان وتضربان الأرض، وكأنها تضربُ المصيرَ الذي لحق بها. لكنها سرعان ما لملمت نفسها.

حين ارتفع أذان العصر، نهضت لتستغفر الله وتصلّي وتتقرَّب إليه حُبّاً فيه، ورهبةً منه. حملت موبايلها على إثر الرنَّة التي نبَّهتها بأنَّ الإنترنت عاد بعد انقطاع مدة أسبوع في مدينة خان يونس. قامت مسرعة تركض، والابتسامة ترتسم على وجهها: "أخيراً جا النت!". بدأت تتفقدً حساباتها الشخصية على "السناب" والإنستغرام" وباقي التطبيقات، تنظر إلى العالم الخارجي كيف يعيش بين الرقص واللعب والتنزُّه، ترسم في مخيلتها صوراً من عودتها إلى هذه الحياة الطبيعية، أو ما يشبهُها، من جديد. استمعت إلى بعض الأغاني. وبتلقائية وعفوية، بدأ خصرها الصغير بالاهتزاز والرقص، لتحرقَ بعض ما أحاط بها من طاقة سلبية، متمايلةً وسط الفصل، مع تصفيق النسوة والأطفال على إيقاع حركاتها، لتشعر بأنها أميرة في فيلم لديزني.

جلست ترتاح قليلاً، بعدما خفَّفت هزّات خصرها من هزّات الصواريخ للأرض من حولهم. تصفَّحت "الإنستغرام"، فإذا بابن عمتها وسيم، في هولندا، نشر "بوستاً"

باللغة الإنجليزية بأنَّ بيت خاله وبيت جدّه دُمِّرا بالكامل، مع صورة لبقايا حجارة وأعمدة محطَّمة وعمارة مكونة من أربعة طوابق تحولت إلى مساحة مفتوحة. استطاعت روزا أنْ تميِّز بقايا بيتها من بين الركام. صرخت:

- بيتنا انقصف . . . دمّروه . . . مو شايفة شي غير الركام!

بدأت تبحث عن غرفة نومها في الصورة لعلَّها تعثر عليها وتطمئن بأن ملابسها وإكسسواراتها وأحذيتها وحقائب اليد التي جلبتها معها من السعودية قبل شهر من بدء العدوان الإسرائيلي سليمة وموجودة. لكنها لم تتمكن من تحديد موقع الغرفة، لأن معالم البيت جميعها اختفت.

ما إن أفرغت روزا بعض الطاقة السلبية التي طوّقتها في الأيام السابقة حتى انهال عليها جبلٌ منها، ليطرحها أرضاً، وتنام بلا وعي، وتستيقظ فجر اليوم التالي، الجمعة، على صوت أختها نسرين تهمس لها:

- شو رأيك نروح على عبسان ونشوف بيوتنا؟

بدون تفكير بما قد تنطوي عليها المغامرة التي ستقوم بها مع شقيقتها من خطورة، أجابتها بـ"نعم" حازمة.

نهضت لتغسل وجهها، وتصلّي صلاة الفجر، وتقرأ القرآن، وتتلو أذكار الصباح، وتدعو الله وتستودعه نفسها وما تملك ليحفظها بحفظه. في الساعة السابعة، انطلقت روزا مع نسرين إلى عبسان الجديدة التي كانت جنَّة على الأرض بأشجارها وورودها وبيوتها الجميلة. ارتدت عباءة سوداء مطرزة باللونين الأزرق والأبيض، وطرحة بيضاء، ونظارة شمسية، وقد أعدّت نفسها للسير مسافةً طويلة، مدركةً بأنها ذاهبة إلى منطقة محظورة، منطقة الموت. ومع ذلك، كان لا بدَّ أن ترى بنفسها.

طوال الطريق، كان لسان روزا يلهج بذكر الله، وقلبها ينبض، على أمل أن تحصل على شيء من مقتنياتها وملابسها، رغم أنها لم تحمل معها حقيبة أو أي شيء تضع فيه ما قد تجده، تتناوب عليها مشاعر متناقضة بين الأمل والخوف، تقطع خطواتٍ جريئةً واثقة، قبل أن يثقل قلبها، فتتباطأ خطواتها توجسّاً.

هذا الإحساس المربك بين النعم واللا أنهكها واستنزفها. بعد ما يقارب الساعتين من الرعب أثناء السير في طريق طويل امتدت على جانبيه أنقاض المباني، وصلت روزا ونسرين إلى عبسان "الجميلة" التي تحولت إلى جبل من ركام. توقفت الأختان بالقرب من كومة حجارة علتها مئذنة، فعرفت روزا أنها كانت تقف بجوار مسجد الفاروق الذي كان يفصل بين مبناها ومبنى شقيقتها نسرين. اتفقتا على أن تتفقد كل واحدة منهما بيتها، على أن تلتقيا بعد الانتهاء من البحث والتنقيب عند المسجد الذي اختفت معالمه.

في البداية، كانت روزا في حالة ضياع، تائهة، لا تستطيع العثور على منزلها، أو ما تبقى منه. بدأت تقيس المسافات بالأشبار، وتحاول أن تستعيد شكل البيوت قبل الهدم، قبل أن تتمكن أخيراً من العثور على العمارة. زكمت أنفها رائحة نتنة، منبعثة من قطيع من الماعز كان قد قُصف أمام العمارة، وقد بدأت الجيف بالتحلل.

جاب بصرها المكان، تبحث عن النعناع والريحان والورود المحيطة بالعمارة، تريد أن تشتمَّ رائحة حياة منعشة لتمسحَ بها رائحة الحيوانات النافقة، لكن للأسف، جميع الورود والرياحين المزروعة أمام العمارة قُصفت. لم يعد هناك جمال، كما لم تعد هناك حياة.

كانت قدماها منهكتين من السير الطويل والمضني. بالكاد كانت قادرة على تسلُّق الركام. دوّى صوت "الزنانة"، الذبابة الحديدية الإسرائيلية، في المكان ليملأه رعباً، إذ لم تكن في المنطقة سوى روزا ونسرين التي كانت هي الأخرى تتفقد منزلها في الجوار.

دخلت روزا بيتها، الذي لم يعد قائماً، بقدمين مُتربتين من آثار غبار الأنقاض، وبدأت بالبحث بين الغرف. أزاحت من طريقها كومة الحجارة التي تعوق حركتها لتصل إلى غرفة نومها، فيما تغلغل غبار الإسمنت الرمادي في ثنايا أظفارها. رأت جدران غرفتها البيضاء قد انهارت على الأرض، وباتت مفتوحةً على بيت الجيران. بطمأنينة وسلام غير متوقعين، ربضت حمامة بيضاء فوق ركام غرفتها.

وقفت في منتصف الغرفة، لا تعرف ماذا تفعل. وقع بصرها على صندوق إكسسواراتها في زاوية الغرفة، فوق الركام، فاندفعت تركض بين الحجارة، غير

آبهة بالخدوش التي لحقت بقدميها، إلى أن تمكنت من الوصول إلى الصندوق. أخذته في حضنها، وعانقته بقوة. تجدَّد الأمل لديها بإمكانية العثور على ملابسها ومقتنياتها، فقرَّرت أن تبدأ من الزاوية اليسرى، مكان خزانتها التي كانت تضم، إلى جانب ملابسها، حقائب اليد من أجود الماركات، وعدداً من لوحاتها الفنية التي تعكس شغفها بالرسم.

رفعت أول طبقة من الحجارة الثقيلة وقلبها ينبض، وعيناها تلمعان، ووجهها يتصبب عرقاً، ويداها الناعمتان يتراكم عليهما السواد.

وجدت ألواحاً خشبية من بقايا خزانة ملابسها. نبشت بقوة، وعلى نحو أسرع، وضربات قلبها تتسارع، حتى رأت ملابسها، كما هي، معلقة ومدفونة تحت الركام. أطلقت صرخة ابتهاج، تداخلت مع صوت "الزنانة" فوق رأسها. لكنّها لم تأبه للأمر. كانت روزا الآن سعيدة جداً. لكن، سرعان ما تغيرت ملامح وجهها البشوش الذي فاض بالتفاؤل إلى ملامح عابسة تملؤها الحسرة لأنها لم تجلب معها شنطة تضع ملابسها فيها. فجأة تذكرت حقائب السفر التي كانت قد وضعتها تحت سريرها، بعد عودتها إلى غزة من السعودية. بدأت تبحث عن الجدار الذي كان السرير يستند إليه، فعثرت عليه، وبدأت تزيح كومة الحجارة وحطام الخشب إلى أن رأت الحقائب ومعها أحذيتها، جميعها تحت ما تبقى من سريرها.

"يا الله ما أعظمك! كم أنت رؤوف بي"، قالت بينها وبين نفسها. الفرحة لم تسعها، فبدأت بجمع ملابسها وأحذيتها واكسسواراتها ومستحضرات التجميل الخاصة بها لتملأ بها أربع حقائب؛ اثنتان بعجلات جرتهما بيديها، واثنتان أخف وزناً تدلتا من كتفيها. هي نفسها كانت مندهشة من القوة الخارقة التي حطَّت في جسدها المتعَب.

وجدت قارورة ماء ملقاة فوق ركام المطبخ، تناولتها وغسلت بها يديها وقدميها. فجأة دوّى انفجار على مسافة قريبة جداً. صرخت، بصوت يرتجف من شدة الخوف: "قصفوا أختي نسرين!".

ارتفع صوت ينادي: "روزا! أنت بخير؟ رُدّي عليّ!"، كانت نسرين. ركضت روزا تحتضنها، وهي تحمد الله. انطلقت الفاشينيستا، بكل ثقة، رأسها مرفوع، وابتسامتها الجميلة تنير وجهها، تجرُّ حقائبها دون أن تشعر بثقل ما تحمله. سارت الشقيقتان مسافة كيلومترين دون أن تجدا وسيلة نقل، إلى أن التقيتا

أربعة شباب، من سكان الحي. لم يُخفِ الشباب دهشتهم من وجود امرأتين في عبسان، منطقة الموت المعلن، تجرجران كل هذه الحقائب. عرضوا على الشقيقتين اللتين كانتا تلهثان من الإنهاك، أن يحملوا عنهما الحقائب ويوصلوها إلى دوار العلَم، في بني سهيلة، كأقرب مكان يمكنهما العثور فيه على وسيلة نقل، كسيارة أو حافلة أو حتى عربة يجرُّها حمار. رافقتهم في سيرهم نسرين، التي كانت حمولتها من "غنائم" بيتها أخف بكثير من حمولة شقيقتها؛ بينما استعارت روزا دراجة هوائية كان أحد الشباب يقودها، مظهرةً جرأة غير معهودة، لتسبقهم عند نقطة الالتقاء.

طارت روزا بـ"البسكليت"، يداعبُ هواء عبسان وجهها. في تلك اللحظة، كانت عبسان هي عبسان الجميلة، حيث لا موت يهطلُ من السماء فجأة، أو يتكدَّسُ في الطرقات. كان هذا أحد أجمل أيام عمرها.

كان المارة في الطريق، يرمقونها بنظرات استغراب، لم تخلُ بعضها من استهجان. قال أحدهم: "إحنا تحت إبادة ولا إيه"، وأضاف آخر: "ما شاء الله! ما شاء الله!"، فيما علَّق ثالث جامعاً بين حس الدعابة والغزل: "شوفوا المُزَّة اللي على البسكليت!".

أخيراً سوف ترتدي روزا ما تحبُّه، وتحتار فيما ترتديه، وستعود فاشينيستا، وستكون جميلة، وستكون هي المرأة التي تعرف.

"هاي أنا!"، صرخت بصوت طال السماء، فيما كانت تسابق الريح.

لتترك لنا غزة شيئاً

نبال النجار

السابع من أكتوبر، الساعة السادسة صباحاً. كنّا نستعدُّ لقطاف الزيتون الذي حان موسمه، كعائلة تترأسُها الجدَّة، فقطاف الزيتون من أجمل مواسم السنة؛ موسم يجمع الأحبَّة في أوقات تتخلَّلها الأهازيج والأناشيد الشعبية مع الشاي والخبز والزعتر، تتحول فيه أيادينا إلى عكازات للجدَّة التي تتقدَّمنا، يسبقُها قلبُها إلى أرضنا في قرية خُزاعة، في خان يونس، ذات الخضرة البهية وتربتها الفواحة بالحياة السخية، وعصافيرها التي تستقبلُنا، إذ تصنع لوحةً تشكيلةً ملونة على خلفية سماء زرقاء شفافة.

حين بدأنا نلملمُ ما يلزم للقطاف والاستعداد للانطلاق سيراً على الأقدام لنستشعرَ جمال اليوم، بدأت ساعة اللعنة.

هكذا تحول ذلك الصباح، من صباحٍ يملؤه الشغف والاستعداد إلى صباح يضجُّ بأصواتٍ مخيفة اخترقت مسامعنا وكادت تُفجِّر عقولنا، فهرولنا متخبِّطين، في محاولة لمعرفة ما كان يدور حولنا، إلى أن تناهى إلى مسامعنا بأن المقاومة اقتحمت غلاف غزة، تلك الأخبار التي تداولتها ألسنة بعض الجيران لأننا لم نستطع حينها الحصول على أي مصدر رسمي يوضح ما كان يحدث.

استمرت تلك الأحداث عدة ساعات، ونحن نشاهدُ بأعيننا ما لم تتخيَّله عقولنا.

تساءلنا ما إذا كانت هذه أهوال يوم القيامة أم لعلَّنا كنا نعيش كابوساً جماعياً. وجدنا أنفسنا نركض، صغاراً وكباراً، تاركين خزاعة وبيوتنا وكل ما يعني لنا شيئاً لنخرج بأرواح سليمة. كانت مشاهد نكبة 1948 تتكرَّر مرة أخرى أمام أعيننا،

هذه المرة كانت نكبتنا نحن، نكبة حيَّة، وليست صوراً أرشيفية أو فيديوهات بالأبيض والأسود الشاحبين.

سبقتنا آلامنا، ومضينا نقتفي دموعنا، عاجزين عن استيعاب العالم من حولنا أو إلى أين نحن ذاهبون. وصلنا إلى بيت أحد أقاربنا، فارتحنا قليلاً، وبدأنا نستجمع أنفاسنا، ورتَّبنا أشياءنا القليلة البسيطة التي استطعنا أنْ نحملها معنا في نزوحنا.

ثم دوّى انفجار قوي أعطانا إشارةً بالنزوح مرة أخرى، فتدفَّق أدرينالين أجسامنا ليرمي بنا في مكانٍ آخر كي نحتمي به ممّا يدور من حولنا. سِرنا مرة أخرى، وخطواتنا تتدافع مع دقات قلوبنا التي كادت من قوتها تمزِّق صدورنا، نحمل حقائب بالية، مليئة بحيواتنا المحطَّمة وأحلامنا المكسورة، فيما كنا نحاول احتواء أطفالنا المعلقين بأجسادنا.

وصلنا محطة نزوح أخرى، نلتمس فيها بقية نَفَس تُعيننا على البقاء. بعد عشرين يوماً من الحفاظ على حياتنا وأنفاسنا، بشق الأنفس، أصدر الجيش الإسرائيلي أوامره بإخلاء المنطقة، ليكون ذلك النزوح الثالث خلال أقل من شهر. فعل الأدرينالين فعله هذه المرة، بكل ما ينطوي عليه من غريزة النجاة، حتى وصلنا إلى محطة جديدة، مدرسة لإيواء الفارين من موتهم المؤجل.

فاض قلبي بالنقمة عندما رأيتُ أطفالاً ونساء ورجالاً يتعاركون على وعاء من الأرز. ذرفتُ طنّاً من الدموع.

كانت مدرسة الإيواء تقع بالقرب من مستشفى ناصر، الكائن في وسط مدينة خان يونس. لم نكن نشعر بانقضاء اليوم بسبب حجم الضجيج والأعداد الهائلة للنازحين. ومع حلول الليل، كنا نعرف أنَّ الموت قادم في أي لحظة، وأنَّ علينا أن نستعدَّ له. كانت صفارات سيارات الإسعاف تزاحمُها أبواق السيارات المسرعة، تنطلق منها صرخات يائسة تدعو إلى إفساح الطريق، إذ كانت تحمل جرحى على أمل إنقاذهم، أطفال ونساء ورجال بُترت أطرافهم، أو قتلى – المحظوظون منهم كاملو الأطراف – أو أشلاء مجهولة الهوية.

كنا نقضي ليالينا ورجفات أجسامنا تنتقل فيما بيننا كالعدوى، ونحن نستمع لتمتمات بعضنا بعضاً بالشهادتين، معتقدين بأنَّ كل يوم هو يومنا الأخير في الحياة.

لم أدرك وقتها أنني كنتُ في نعمة لم أُقدِّر قيمتها إلى أن ذهبتُ إلى قسم الإصابات في المستشفى أبحث عن مكان أتوضّأ فيه من أجل صلاة المغرب، بسبب شحّ المياه في المدرسة؛ إذ رأيتُ رجلاً سحقه الحزن، كان يجلس مهزوماً أمام قلَّة حيلته. بدا كما لو أن جزءاً من قلبه قد بُتر. كان يبكي ابنته ذات الأربعة أعوام التي استلقت غائبة عن الوعي على سرير متقشِّف، ينظر إليها نظرة العاجز. لم أسمع سوى دعائه بصوت خافت وبيده مسبحة: "الرجاء منك يا الله، والشفاء منك يا الله، أنت ربُّ المستضعفين يا الله".

لم أتمالك دموعي حينها. لا أعلم دموع ماذا تحديداً؛ هل هي دموع إشفاق على الأب العاجز أم على البنت التي سلبها صاروخ إسرائيلي حاقد ساقها وذراعها؟ كانت جميلة جداً، ككل الأطفال في مثل عمرها، ولعلها كانت تريد أن تفيق من غيبوبتها بسرعة، كي تلهو مع رفيقاتها. قاومتُ رغبتي بتمسيد شعرها الحريري الأشقر الذي انسدل على جانبي وجهها الصغير. تخيَّلتُ أمَّها تمشِّطه وتبكي، وهي تؤكد لها أنه مهما يكن ستبقى دائماً جميلة.

شعرتُ أيضاً بنعمة الجسد المعافى – على الأقل حتى اللحظة.

عدتُ إلى مأواي البائس محطَّمةً من هول المشهد. في الليل، بكيت. دموعي هطلت بغزارة.

ظللتُ أستعيد المشهد في ذهني مراراً وتكراراً، وأنا أكابد لمواساة أطفالي، وتوفير الطعام لهم، وتلبية احتياجاتهم، تلك المسؤوليات التي من المفترض أن يتكفل والدهم بها. لكنّه كان قد غادر غزة قبل أسبوعين من ذلك اليوم المشؤوم، إذ سافر إلى الخارج طلباً للعمل، ليؤمّن لنا لقمة العيش.

سارت أيامنا على ذلك المنوال. انقضت ثلاثة أشهر من مرارة العيش حين دقَّت ساعة النزوح الرابعة إلى محطة أخرى، اعتقدنا آنذاك أنها آخر محطة للتنفس، قبل أن أجد نفسي في خيمة، أنا وأطفالي وجدَّتهم وعمّهم، ومن حولنا عدد كبير من النازحين في خلاء مقفر، مخيف.

اليوم، بعد أربعة أشهر من المعاناة في المخيم أحاول أن أكتب، علَّ الكلمات تخفِّف قليلاً مما حُفر في قلوبنا من حزن وفقد؛ فقد الناس، وفقد البيت، وفقد الأماكن، وفقد غزة، وفقد العالم الذي كنا نعرفه.

آلاف القصص، وآلاف البيوت الباردة بلا أهلها، وآلاف الأحضان الفارغة، جميعها ستكون جزءاً من ذاكرة مدينة، تُفجع في هذا العالم وحدَها، وتتألمُ وحدَها، وتموتُ وحدَها أيضاً.

لم أعد أريد أن أكون جزءاً من فجيعة غزة وجحيمها، فلتمُت هي وحدها.

لكن، لتترك لنا جذراً، وساقاً خضراء، وأرضاً طيِّبة، وهواءً مشاكساً، وبحراً متقلب المزاج، وماءً من بئر الذاكرة، وطفلاً يضحك ويلهو ويشاغب، وقلباً يخفق بالحبِّ الأول، وزمناً قادماً.

رحلوا

مرام حمو

الظلام المتقطّع كان يلفُّ المخيم، لكن ذلك لم يُضفِ عليه طابع السكون، فالناس لم يكونوا نياماً؛ أضواء باهتة كانت تشعُّ من بيوتهم المتراصَّة بعصبية. كنّا نبيتُ أربع عائلات معاً في ليلة غير عادية وسط وابل من الصواريخ. كان الخوف هو الطاغي. أصوات الانفجارات العنيفة لم تهدأ للحظة، ومع كل انفجار كانت الأرض تتزلزل، تكاد السماء تنطبق عليها.

كان المنزل يتأرجح، وقد سمعنا تساقط حجارة وزجاج وشظايا، حيث تهيّأ لنا بأن الصواريخ تسقط على رؤوسنا، ثم انتشرت رائحة البارود والرماد والذكريات. تطايرت قطعة القماش المهترئة التي علّقناها عوضاً عن شباك البيت الذي اقتلعته انفجارات سابقة من جذره. انحنى الجميع، وتعالت صرخات الخوف من الأطفال، وأحياناً من الكبار.

سمعتُ دقات قلبي السريعة، رغم أنه مع كل انفجار كانت تُصمُّ أذناي. لا أستطيع أن أحصي عدد المرات التي أغمضتُ فيها عينيّ، ثم فتحتهما مرة أخرى لأتأكد بأن لا شيء انهار حولي، وأنَّ مشاهد سبق وأنْ عشتُها لم تتكرَّر هنا. تمالكتُ نفسي، وتظاهرتُ بأنني قوية، فيما كنتُ أحاول طمأنة الخائفين، مؤكدةً لهم بأنّ القصف بعيد، وأنّ علينا الاستعانة بالله والتوكل عليه، فهو الحافظ.

صوت انفجار آخر قطع الطريق إلى قلبي فارتجف. سرت في جسدي قشعريرة. هذه المرة كان وقْعُ الانفجار مختلفاً، كأنه اقتلع روحي. شعرتُ بأنه نذير شؤم، لكنني هوَّنتُ على نفسي ومَن حولي كالعادة.

حلَّ الفجر.

قطع صوت موبايل أبي صمت الحاضرين. توجسَّت قلوبُنا. "ألوو! مين؟ متى؟! لا حول ولا قوة إلا بالله". توجهت أبصارنا نحو أبي، نحاول أن نتبيَّن ما جرى. كلماته القليلة المشدوهة أنبأت بأن أحدهم قُتل. رغم أن ما يضمره القلب من أحزان قد يكون أضعاف ما تبديه قسمات الوجه، لكن ما أظهرته تجاعيد جبين أبي والعرق الغزير الذي سال منه روى ما حدث ببلاغة مميتة، أضعافاً مضاعفة.

انتهت المكالمة التي خُيِّل لنا أنها استمرت دهراً بأكمله. كنّا ننتظر التفاصيل. نظرنا جميعاً إلى أبي بعيون مليئة بالاستفسار، وألسنتا مكبَّلة، غير قادرين على النطق بسؤال: "مين؟". قال أبي بكلماتٍ متقطعة وصوت يرتجف وعيون تحبس دموع قهرٍ وحزن بأن منزل عمتي المأهول بالأحباب قُصف.

ارتسم الذهول على وجوهنا، كأنما الزمن توقف. كانت صدمتي تجلس بجواري كظل ثقيل. تداعى جسدي، وجفّت الدموع من عيني، واحتُبست الكلمات في صدري. كلما حاولتُ أن أفتح فمي، انكمشت كلماتي في جوف الحزن ومزّقت روحي. تساؤلات غير مجابة دارت في رأسي، كأنني في عالم مظلم يسحبني عميقاً.

لماذا قتلوا عمَّتي؟

لماذا سلبوني عينيها الحانيتين؟

من سيعوض حضنها الفخور بي في أوقات نجاحي؟

كيف سأعيش من غير أن أسمع اسمي بصوتها؟

لماذا يجب أن أخسر القلب الذي أحبُّه؟

عمَّتي الحبيبة كانت أملي وداعمتي في كل خطواتي، وسندي في دراستي في كلية الطب، لطالما كانت تنتظر أن أتخرج طبيبة. كانت تخبرني دوماً بأنها تثق بي، وبأنني سأكون رقماً صعباً في العالم. بموتها العنيف، شعرتُ بأنني أدفن حلمي معها.

رحيلها كسر قلبي، مزّق شيئاً في داخلي، لا أعرف له اسماً أو وصفاً، لكنني شعرتُ بانطفاءة في صدري، هكذا دفعة واحدة.

لدقائق ضجّت أصوات من حولي، أحدهم كان يطرح أسئلة تفصيلية، وآخر كان يحاول أن يعرف من قُتِل في القصف. تداخلت الأصوات بارتباك وذعر، ثم خفتت تدريجياً، كما لو أنَّ الحقيقة بدأت تتسلل إلينا من قلب السكون الثقيل، الذي خيَّم على المكان، كالقبر المفتوح الذي يلتهم ما تبقى من أمان وحياة.

جلستُ بين الوجوه المقهورة من حولي، أتأمل ملامحهم المتجهِّمة التي تراوحت بين الصدمة والإنكار وعدم التصديق. كنتُ وحيدة، كأقصى ما يمكن أن تكون عليه الوحدة. كنتُ كالمغشي عليها، أنتظر بقية الخبر، فالخبر للأسف لا يأتي دفعةً واحدة، بل يكون على هيئة جرعات متتالية من الألم والحسرة، لتهدَّ كاهلَ المرء على دفعات.

عمَّتي رحلت.

زوجها، وبناتها، وأبناؤها، وأحفادها، وكنائنها، وأنسباؤها. ومعارفها رحلوا.

أقارب آخرون لنا رحلوا.

جيراننا رحلوا.

بيتنا وكل ما فيه رحل.

الحيُّ وملامحه وناسه رحلوا.

جميعهم رحلوا.

إسكافي الحرب

سامية اللحام

ذابت الأيام، وتداخلت فيما بينها. أصبحنا لا نُميّز أيام الأسبوع. كلُّ الأفعال والأخبار كانت مكرَّرة حدّ التماثل التام. المجازر هي، هي. صراخ الأطفال وبكاؤهم هو، هو. الموت لم يفارق هذه المدينة، بات رفيقاً يومياً، وأصبحنا نستقبل كلَّ شيء بلا مبالاة.

في طريق عودتي من "جمعية الثقافة والفكر الحر"، إحدى المساحات الآمنة القليلة في غزة، إلى المكان الذي نزحنا إليه، كنتُ أبحث عن "مصلِّح أحذية". كانت حرارة الجو لا تُطاق، وكان العرق يتصبَّب مني بغزارة.

اضطررتُ إلى السير مسافةً طويلةً إلى أن استدللتُ عليه أخيراً بعد عناء؛ رجل كبير في السن، ذو لحية طويلة يكسوها الشيب، كان يُغطي رأسه بقطعة قماش مهترئة لونها أحمر، وقد لاحت على وجهه تجاعيد الحزن والقهر، لا الكِبر. جلس على مقعد خشبي يخيط فردة حذاء، تحيط به من حوله شباشب وأحذية بالية. لم يكن في الأساس "إسكافياً"، لكن ظروف الحرب القاسية أجبرته على أن يجلس على هذا المقعد البشع، وأن يصبح إسكافياً ليُعيل عائلته.

خاطبتُه بخجل:

- يعطيك العافية. ممكن بعد إذنك تخيطلي الحذاء هاد؟ ترى إنت بتعرف الوضع.. ما في أحذية بالبلد.

أجابني بصوت متقطع، دون أن يرفع رأسه:

- حاضر ولا يهمك. بس بدّك تستنّي الدور.

هززتُ رأسي قائلة:

- ماشي . . . بستنّا . . . بس بقديش بتعملو يا عمّو؟

أجابني مازحاً:

- بمئة شيكل.

ضحكتُ وقلتُ له:

- أنا كريمة وأنت بتستاهل.. حلّت البركة!

قال لي بامتنان:

- الله يعطيكِ ويوفقك يا بنتي.

انتظرتُ نصف ساعة تقريباً، مع الواقفين في الدور، والشمس تضربُ رؤوسنا. كانت المنطقة مزدحمة بالنازحين. كان الباعة الجائلون يعرضون بضائعهم، أصواتهم تملأ المكان من كل صوب، فيما اخترق الفضاء صوت صافرة سيارة الإسعاف، منبهةً الناس: "افسحوا الطريق! لدينا مصاب حالته خطيرة".

حين جاء دوري أخيراً، قام إسكافي الحرب بخياطة الجزء العلوي الممزَّق من حذائي، مثبِّتاً إياه بالنعل. لم يستغرق منه الأمر وقتاً طويلاً، كما لو أنَّه كان يمتهن هذه الحرفة طوال حياته. رفع رأسه ونظر إليّ، وقد اسودَّ وجهه واحترق من لهيب الشمس؛ عيناه متورِّمتان، محمّرتان كالجمر، طافحتان بالدموع؛ ويداه الهرمتان والمتشقِّقتان كانتا ترتجفان من شدة التعب.

قال لي بصوت متكسِّر:

- والله يا بنتي بعد ما استشهدوا بناتي الاثنين البكرات، أول فرحتي، وفقدت بيتي، ما عاد يفرق معي لا مصاري ولا أملاك ولا حتى نفسي.

ثم انهمرت دموعُه الحبيسة على وجهه.

تمزقتُ من الوجع في داخلي، ولم أتمالك السيطرة على دموعي التي هطلت بغزارة. استجمعتُ نفسي وقلتُ له:

- الله يرحمهم يا عمو ويعوضك خير، بكرة انشاء لله بكونو شفيعات إلك، والحمد لله على كل حال.

هزَّ رأسه، متمتماً:

- الحمد لله!

أخذتُ الحذاء، ومددتُ عليه النقود، فتعفَّف قائلاً:

- لا يا بنتي . . . ما بدي فلوس.

لكنني أصررتُ عليه:

- لا والله! حقَّك لازم تاخذو.

وافق بعد إلحاح من جانبي. ودَّعته، محاولةً أنْ أبدو متماسكة أمامه:

- تزعلش يا عمو! الدنيا فانية، وكلنا على نفس الطريق.

مشيتُ مبتعدة، مطأطأةً رأسي. لم أشأ أن يراني أحد وأنا أبكي.

طابور الخبز

علي أبو زايد

كانت ليلةً هادئةً من ليالي الإبادة على قطاع غزة. الساعة كانت تشير إلى الثالثة والنصف فجراً. كنتُ غارقاً في النوم الذي انحرمنا منه لأيام كثيرة منذ بدء الحرب، حين أيقظتني زوجتي، مهجة القلب، بصوت خافت:

علي! علي! قوم عشان تروح على المخبز، تصف في الدور، وبس ترجع بتنام، بعينك الله!

نظرتُ إليها، ونهضتُ من الفراش، وأنا أقول في داخلي: "حتى النوم بدناش نتهنّى فيه". ذهبتُ إلى الحمام كي أغتسل وأتوضأ، وإذ بالمياه مقطوعة. تذكرتُ أنني لم أقُم بملء خزان المياه لأن (أبو جميل)، صاحب شاحنة نقل المياه، الذي نشتري منه حاجتنا من الماء، لم يأتِ بالأمس، ومياه البلدية مقطوعة عن الحي منذ فترة بسبب نقص الوقود. استخدمتُ قنينة مياه للشرب كي أتوضأ، ثم ارتديتُ ملابسي، وذهبتُ إلى المخبز الذي لم يكن يبعد كثيراً عن المنزل.

رغم الهدوء النسبي، إلا أن الحذر والخوف سيطرا عليّ. سرّعتُ الخطو كي أحجز دوراً في مقدمة طابور الخبز، على أمل أن أعود مبكراً لاستكمال جرعة النوم. حين وصلت، كان الطابور قد امتلأ فعلياً بالناس، لكنني قلتُ في نفسي: "لا بأس، لم يكن هناك عدد كبير أمامي. سوف أنتظر الحاج ذياب، صاحب المخبز، الذي سيوزع علينا بطاقات أرقام لتحديد دور كل منّا في الطابور".

كانت السماء صافية والجو دافئاً بعض الشيء، وكان الشباب الذين وقفوا في الطابور يتحدثون عن الأوضاع والأحوال التي وصلنا إليها، ومعاناة الناس، والإبادة التي طالتنا جميعاً. مع رفع آذان الفجر، صليتُ في الشارع لأحافظ على مكاني في الطابور، قبل أن أعود لمواصلة الحديث مع الشباب. كان هناك شاب غريب عن منطقتنا،

لم أره من قبل في الحي الذي نسكن فيه. كان طويل القامة، قمحي اللون، شعره طويل وأشعث كأنه لم يحلقه منذ فترة. اسمه فيصل. كان يتحدث عن معاناة نزوحه، فهو من سكان مدينة غزة، لكن الإبادة أجبرته على النزوح إلى الجنوب. أخذ يحدثني عن الصعوبات التي واجهته وهو في طريقه إلى الجنوب، وكنتُ مندمجاً في تفاصيل قصته تماماً، حتى إنّني لم أعد أستمع لأحاديث شباب الحي.

روى لي فيصل تفاصيل مروّعة لتجربة مؤلمة خاضها، حين اضطر عند نزوحه مع زوجته وابنه إلى التوقف عند " "الحلابة" – وهي نقطة تفتيش أقامها الجيش الإسرائيلي للغزيين الفارين. استعاد فيصل مرارة ما حدث قائلاً:

- عندما جاء دوري في المرور، طلب مني الجندي الإسرائيلي الوقوف إلى اليسار. جميع من كان يتم إيقافهم، يختبرون كل أنواع الإذلال والألم والقهر. جاء جندي يتحدث العربية. طلب مني هويتي، ثم أمرني بأن أخلع ملابسي.

سكت الشاب الغزي للحظات، والدموع في عينيه. قلتُ له بصوت خافت وبدن مقشعر:

- هل خلعتَها كلها؟

- كلها بلا تردد. فأنا أعلم أنَّ أي تردُّد أو رفض كان يمكن أن يكلفني حياتي.

وتابع، مستعيداً المشهد بنبرة طفحت بالأسى:

- خلعتُ ملابسي قطعة، قطعة، وأنا أرتجف خوفاً، وأبقيتُ فقط على سروالي الداخلي "البوكسر".

كان طابور الخبز قد استطال كثيراً. وبدأ الشباب يتدافعون للحصول على دور فيه. تجنَّبتُ المزاحمة في الطابور لأن الحاج ذياب لم يأتِ بعد لتوزيع بطاقات الأرقام علينا. كان تركيزي منصبّاً لمعرفة ما حدث مع فيصل، الذي واصل:

- قيَّد الجندي يديَّ إلى الخلف، وعصَّب عينيّ، وأنا جالس على ركبتي، ثم تركني. بدأتُ أفكر: ماذا سيحصل؟ هل سيعتقلونني؟ هل سيقتلونني؟ هل سيطلقون سراحي؟

ارتسم الغمّ على وجه فيصل، الذي ابتلع غصَّة، وقد تحشرج صوته، قبل أن يتابع:

- لكن التفكير الأكبر كان في زوجتي وطفلي الذي لم يبلغ الأربعة أعوام؛ فقد عبرا "نقطة الحلابة" بعدي. زوجتي لم تكن تعرف شيئاً في مناطق الجنوب، فهي من مدينة غزة. بقيتُ في وضعية الركوع نفسها، لفترة بدت لي أزلية. لم أستطع أن أتحرك بأي شكل من الأشكال خوفاً من أن ألقى مصير غيري من الشباب الذين تم اعتقالهم من قبل.

توقف قليلاً مستجمعاً أفكاره، وقال:

- لا أعرف كم من الوقت انقضى وأنا على هذه الحال، إلى أن جاء الجندي وأعطاني الهوية ورفع العصبة عن عينيّ وفكَّ قيدي وأمرني بالذهاب فوراً إلى الجنوب. حملتُ ملابسي وانطلقت راكضاً، دون أن ألتفت إلى الوراء. قطعتُ المسافة كلها وأنا شبه عار، أمام أفواج النازحين، رجالاً ونساء وأطفالاً، قبل أن أتمكن من ارتداء ملابسي.

حرص فيصل على أن يحدثني عن مشهد عريه وسط النازحين بصوت خافت، خشية أن يسمعه الشباب في الطابور، واضعاً يده على فمه.

ومضى يقول:

- وبدأتُ رحلة البحث عن زوجتي وابني. سحبتُ موبايلي من جيب البنطلون وحاولت الاتصال بزوجتي، دون أن أتلقى أي ردّ.

في الأثناء، كان صاحب المخبز قد وصل، وبدأ يوزع بطاقات الدور على الشباب الواقفين في الطابور، للتخفيف من التدافع والفوضى. كانت قد مرّت ساعات وأنا أنتظر في الطابور. أخذتُ الرقم وعدتُ لفيصل، دون أن يحيد انتباهي عن متابعة قصته. وإذ بصوت انفجار ضخم ملأ دويُّه المكان. انطلقت صرخات متلاحقة: "إسعاف.. إسعاف". لم نعلم من أين أتت الصرخات. تغلَّفت السماء بالغبار، ولم نعد نرى شيئاً.

حين بدأت سحبُ الغبار والدخان تتبدَّد أخيراً، أخذنا نتفقَّد بعضنا بعضاً مذعورين، فيما تراكض الناس، يبحثون عن أبنائهم الذين كانوا في طابور الخبز،

ومعظمهم من الشباب والفتية والأطفال. صوت سيارة الإسعاف كان يعلو من بعيد. حاولتُ أن أستجمع نفسي لأستوعب ما حصل.

تبين أنّ طائرات الإبادة الإسرائيلية قصفت منزلاً مجاوراً للمخبز. هرعت زوجتي إلى المكان مسرعة، تبحث عني، لتأخذني بين ذراعيها، وأنا مكسو بالغبار بالكامل. كنتُ أستطيع أن أسمع دقات قلبها تخفق برعب، وهي تقول فيما كانت تمسح الغبار بيدها الدافئة عن وجهي:

- الحمد لله يا عمري إنك بخير. خلص تعال روِّح! بدناش خبز!

عيناي جالتا الوجوه من حولي، جميعها كانت مغبرَّة. كنتُ أبحث عن فيصل. لا أعتقد أنه أكمل رواية قصَّته.

حبل سُري

ميساء سلامة

هي أوقاتٌ عجاف، يتعانق فيها الفراق واللقاء بحرقة. رائحة الغبار تمتزج بأنفاس الانتظار. الصوت المخيف للقصف وانهيار المباني يدوّي في الأفق.

يشتدُّ الزحام، فيمسكُ يدَها كأغنيةٍ ضاق بها الطريق، ويجذبُ صغيرتهما المشاكسة نحوه لتظلَّ قريبةً، فلا تفلت منه. لا يسمعُ إلا ما يراه بعينيه من خوف، والقليل من الكلمات التي يسرقها من حركة شفاه الناس، محاولاً أن يقرأ ما يدور حوله.

يُنادي ضابط جيش الاحتلال بصوته المنفِّر:

- النساء والأطفال . . . تقدَّموا! والشباب للخلف!

يهبطُ الليل على قلبها وهي تسمع. تبكي وتنظر إلى زوجها، ثم تناوله وليدتهما في قماطها، وتحدِّثه بيديها المرتعشتين، وتترجم له ما يقوله الضابط بلغة الإشارة.

يتتبَّع لغة يديها، ويطوِّقُها بنظرة حانية. من وسط مسير الناس بهيئاتهم الذاهلة، لا يرى إلا زوجته بعينيها العسيلتين الباكيتين ووجهها الطفولي الصبوح الذي شاخ فجأة. تُرخي جفونها، وتميل عليه، وتُنهنه. تتكئ بكل ثقلها على آخر ما تبقى لها من وقت.

هي لحظة الفراق إذن.

يُعيد لها الرضيعة، وعرقه يتصبَّبُ من وجهه. يخلع حقيبة الظهر، التي كان يحملها طيلة طريق النزوح المضني، والتي تضم بعض الاحتياجات الضرورية؛

من حفاضات، وملابس، ومستلزمات النظافة الأساسية، إلى جانب أوراق العائلة الثبوتية. يساعدها في تثبيتها على ظهرها برفق، وهو يشعر بالعجز المضاعف؛ إذ لم يعد بمقدوره الآن أن يكون معها، سنداً ويداً وعوناً وصبراً، يخفِّف عنها شيئاً من العبء، ويحميها ويحمي طفلتيهما. يقول لها بلغة يديه اللتين تتضاربان وترتجفان:

- لازم تتقدمي وتتشجعي! ما بدّي أفقد البنتين ولا أفقدك. كوني قوية! يلّا تحرَّكي!

بغيمةٍ من الدموع، تستمعُ إلى يديه، وهي تقول في داخلها: "كيف بس أتركك لحالك؟ ما حد بعرف إنك ما راح تسمع، وسمّاعتك مش معك، وأنا بقدرش، إذا بدّي أموت بس أموت بحبك. شو فايدة الحياة وأنت مش معي؟".

تستمر محاولاته بإقناعها. وأخيراً، بملامح متعبة وبقلب كحبَّة جوز يابسة توافقه تحت وطأة الضغط منه للنجاة بحياتها وحياة طفلتيهما. يُخرج قلماً من جيبه، ويكتب اسم ابنتهما الكبرى "مستكة" على يدها، ثم يربط معصمها بمعصم أمّها بحبل، وكأنه حبل سُرّي آخر يوفر لها الأمان خارج الرحم مرَّةً ثانية بعد ثلاثة أعوام من الميلاد، فلا تضيع في الطريق، أو تفقد الأمان في بطن هذا الكابوس.

تبكي بمرارة. يغمرهن بين ذراعيه، فيصبحن ثلاثتهن موسيقى في حضنه. في محاولة منه كي يضمد جراح دمعه، يخاطبها بيديه وعينيه:

- طعميني الخبز من ابتسامتك. بدأت أشعر بالجوع يا حلوتي. بحبك، وعندي ثقة فيكي.

يقفُ ظلاً منكسراً، وينحني ليُقبِّل مستكة:

- بابا! ربطت إيدك بإيد ماما. أخاف على فراشتنا تطير وتبعد عن الماما. انتبهي على ماما.

بإيقاع بطيء وحركة ثقيلة، تمشي، تاركةً قلبَها وراءها، تتملَّكُها مشاعرُ رعبٍ وهي تجرُّ صغيرتها بالحبل السُّري الجديد، وتضمُّ رضيعتها إلى صدرها، والموت يحلِّقُ فوقهن كالنسر، ورائحته تستولي على الشهيق والزفير.

تتقدَّم، وتذوب في السيل البشري بين وابل التهديدات من الجنود المتغطرسين وخوفها على فقدان صغيرتها وسط زحام الأقدام المتدافعة. تشتدُّ عقدة الحبل حول معصم مستكة، فتوجع يدها الصغيرة مع كل جذب، فيما تبكي رضيعتها على صدرها وكأنها تُطلق صرخة الموت بعد صرخة الحياة قبل أيام. تُثبِّتها إلى اليسار قليلاً، حيث قلبها. بكاؤها يزداد حدَّة. تنظر إليها بدمع العاجزة عن رضاعتها، يتآكلها القهر. تهمسُ لها كأنها معتذرة: "بعرف أنك جوعانة، لكن ما بيدي شيء يا صغيرتي". تبكي مستكة، فيزداد توتُّرها من طفلتيها، ومن دموعهما.

تصلُ مع الصغيرتين إلى الحاجز الأول، أو ما يسمّونه مجازاً "حَلّابَة". تكاد الحقيبة التي ينوء بها ظهرها تقسمه إلى نصفين. ثقلها يجعل مطراً ينتظر في رحم الغيم أن يهطل بين ساقيها. تتساءل: هل انسكب اللون الأحمر على الأرض؟ يقطع خوفها صراخ جندي، يأمر السيدات بالجلوس على الأرض ورفع الأيدي. الأرض تضيق بها. تلتفت، فترى الدموع تنزف من العيون، والترقُّب سيد الموقف. صوت الإهانة يعلو. تجلس النساء متجاورات بصمت، كأنهن توابيت، ينتظرن العبور.

دقائق ويأمرهن جندي لعين بالوقوف. تحاول أن تستجمع قوتها. تقف، وتشدُّ الحبل، وتتلمَّس بطنها الذي لم يتخلَّص من آثار الولادة تماماً، وتتحسَّس ثيابها خجلاً.

يعاود الجندي إصدار أوامره بصوته الغليظ:

- ارفعن أيديكن بالهويات!

ترفعُ الهوية باليد المربوطة بيد مستكة، محدثةً نفسها فيما كانت تعتصر رسغ صغيرتها: "يا الله ليش لازم نموت مرات كتيرة قبل موتنا النهائي؟ هل حياتنا تحت رحمة نزوة عابرة لجندي عابر؟".

تشدُّ مستكة الحبل لأسفل، وهي تبكي:

- يا ماما ما راح أطير. لا تشدّي الحبل لفوق! إيدي وجعتني. وين بابا يحملني؟ ما بدي الحبل.

تخمش كلمات مستكة صدرها، فتبلع ريقها، وكأن حجراً علق في حنجرتها. تشد الحبل برفق، كي تُقرِّب ابنتها إليها أكثر. تسأل نفسها وهي ترتعدُ من الخوف: "شو دخل بناتي بكل هالجنون؟ ليش إحنا الشعب الوحيد إلّي بنعطيهم الحياة من الختام؟".

يتلفَّت الجميع لنداءات الحذر. تقف وكأنها على المقصلة، ثم يعاود الجندي السماح للجميع بالمرور. تتفقَّد اللون الأحمر والحبل. تنظر إلى رضيعتها التي لا تتوقف عن البكاء. تشعر بدوار. تتقدم إلى الأمام بين النسوة والأطفال؛ لا فرق الآن بين طفلة صغيرة يعتريها الذعر، وامرأة يرتسم العجز والوهن في تجاعيد وجهها.

تحاول أن تصمد، لكنها تفقد وعيها. تفتح عينيها، وحولها بعض النسوة اللاتي يحاولن إيقاظها. تنادي:

- بناتي!

تضع امرأة رضيعتها بين ذراعيها، فتحضنها وتشمُّ رائحة بياض الحليب، كأنها تستنشق رائحة الطمأنينة. أما مستكة، فتدور حولها بالحبل، كزهرة عباد الشمس، ثم تقفز وتعانقها، قائلة:

- يا ماما كنتِ راح تطيري لولا الحبل. مسكتك منه وشدّيتك. راح أحكي لبابا.

تُناولها سيدة مسنَّة بضع قطرات من المياه، تنظر إليها، وهي نفسها تجهش بالبكاء، وتقول لها:

- يا بنتي الكل خسران في لعبة الموت الّي بنعيشها، الشاطر إلّي بكون محظوظ وبعيش بأقل الخسائر، أنا تركت وراي أولادي، وهم رصيدي للزمن وعكازي في الكبر، ولكن لطف الله غالب، قومي رضعي الصغيرة.

تُطبطب كلمات العجوز على قلبها، فتنهض للبحث عن مكان ساتر لرضاعة طفلتها. تقف، فيما تشمُّ رائحة الدماء على الأرض وعلى ثيابها، وتبكي بحرقة أكبر.

تضمُّ صغيرتها إليها، وتجلس بجوار بقايا عربة متهالكة من القصف لترضعها، وهي تفكر بزوجها: "يا ترى شو صار معه؟ معقول يحكوا معه وما يرد، فيطلقوا عليه الرصاص".

أسئلة كثيرة تتصارع في رأسها. من سيقنع عدواً جائراً أنه لا يسمع، وأنه فقد سمّاعته الصغيرة التي كانت تطنُّ في رأسه من ذبذبات طائراتهم المسيَّرة؟ هل مصيره السجن والتعذيب؟ أم الموت؟ العدو جعله يغوص في محيط من الصمت غير صامت.

لكن الحب قوي، كالموت.

الحكاية لم تنته

سماح أبو عواد

عندما خطت قدماي مدرسة للإيواء، كانت قد استقبلتْ أعداداً كبيرة من النازحين الهاربين من الرعب معتقدين بأن المدارس أكثر أماناً، تلفتُّ حولي، يميناً ويساراً، لعلّي أجد بقعة، أي مساحة صغيرة، تتَّسع لي ولمتاعي القليل.

كان هناك أطفال يصرخون من شدة الذعر، عدد منهم يبحثون عمن تبقّى من أهاليهم؛ وامرأة تبكي على فقدان ابنها؛ ورجال، من بينهم مسنّون، توزَّعوا في أي حيز متاح، وجوههم منقبضة. واصلتُ بحثي عن مكان يحتويني. كانت الصفوف الدراسية مكتظَّة، والممرات مزدحمة بالأطفال، منهم من كانوا يلعبون، وآخرون جلسوا بصمت، ملامح وجوههم لم تعد تشبه الطفولة.

دخلتُ غرفةَ صف تغصُّ بالنساء وأطفالهن وضوضاء صراخهم وبكائهم، حقائب وأمتعة ارتمت في كل زاوية. لمحتُ بقعةً في منتصف الصف، تُركت خاليةً كممر. احتللتُها على الفور، وجلستُ على الأرض مع حقائبي أنتظر دقّات قلبي تهدأ. لم تتجاوز مساحة بقعتي متراً مربعاً، فأطبقت عليَّ بضيقها. اتخذتُ وضعية القرفصاء، ومسحتُ ببصري أرجاء الصف لعلّي أجد وجهاً مألوفاً. جميعهم كانوا وجوهاً غريبة، لكننا جميعنا حملنا الثقل نفسه، والهموم نفسها.

بدأتُ أشعر بالاختناق. ضاقت أنفاسي. احتجتُ إلى أن ألتقط نسمة هواء. توجهتُ بلهفة ناحية شباك الصف. أغمضتُ عيني، واستنشقتُ الهواء بعمق، لكن أنفاسي امتلأت بغبار القصف العالق في الجو، فسعلت. عدتُ إلى بقعتي الصغيرة أبحثُ عن شربة ماء في إحدى حقائبي.

استيقظتُ مبكراً على ضجيج الأطفال، بعضهم كانوا يلعبون وآخرون يبكون. كانت النساء يدردشن فيما كان الرجال في الممر، خارج غرفة الصف، يتداولون آخر

الأخبار. كان الصداع ينهش رأسي من الألم. نهضتُ من مكاني بصعوبة لأبحث عن الماء لأغسل وجهي، لعلّي أستعيد بعض قوتي ونشاطي حتى أستطيع الوقوف في طابور المساعدات الغذائية، للحصول على وجبة طعام لا تسدُّ الجوع. لكن مثلما يقولون: "ريحة البر ولا عدمه".

وقفتُ في الطابور الطويل أنتظرُ دوري. وقعت مشاجرة بين امرأتين بسبب تعدّي إحداهما على دور الأخرى. بعد ساعات لا نهاية لها من الانتظار، أصيب فيها جسدي بالخدر، جاء دوري أخيراً، واستلمتُ حصتي من الطعام التي كانت عبارة عن علبة جبنة، وعلبة فول، وفقط.

غادرتُ زاوية البؤس الجماعي تلك، أحاول أن أقنع نفسي بأن هذه ليست الحياة الحقيقية. هذا ليس واقعنا.

زحف النهار بطيئاً، وثقيلاً، قبل أن يسقط الليل، لتبدأ معه معاناة من نوع آخر. السؤال الأساسي الذي أرّق النازحين: كيف سننام؟ تبعه سؤال آخر: أين سنضع فراشنا؟

عن نفسي، لم أفكر بكيف وأين. تكورتُ على نفسي، منهكة من شدة التعب، تعب النزوح والفقدان – فقدان الأرواح، والدار، والأحلام، والماضي، والحاضر، وما قد يأتي.

كانت هناك لحظة سكون في الكون سريعة الأفول، تمثّلت في الصمت العابر بين قصفٍ وقصف، وسط هدأة الأجساد النائمة والمستنزفة؛ وهي لحظة أضاءت فيها أحلامي البعيدة. كانت حقيقية جداً. غفوتُ على إحساس جميل بأنني سوف أستيقظ في داري، محاطةً بأشيائي التي أحب، بأهلي، وحياتي، وذكرياتي، وحكاياتي التي سأكتبها يوماً ما.

من أجل الحفاضات

عبدالله السيد

بائعٌ متجول كان يصرخُ بأعلى صوته:

كيس البامبرز بـ 240 شيكل!

للمرة الخامسة، ذهبتُ إلى السوق ولم أجد حفاضات أطفال بسعر معقول، يناسب دخلي المتدني، الذي تدنّى كثيراً مع العدوان الإسرائيلي. لم أدّخر أي طريقة لطرق أبواب المؤسسات الداعمة ووكالة الغوث للاجئين لتوفير الحفاضات وحليب الأطفال بشكل مجاني، لكن في كل مرة، كانت كرامتي تتبعثر ونفسي تتداعى من عجزي المستمر في توفير أدنى مقومات الحياة.

كنتُ قد تلقيتُ أمس اتصالاً من سيّدة، تربطني بها معرفة، وتعرف أنني أعمل مع مؤسسات أهليّة تقدم مساعدات إنسانية. شكت لي ظروفها القاهرة، وسألتني، والحياء يغلبُ على صوتها، ما إذا كنتُ أستطيع أن أؤمّن حفاضات لطفلها. حاولتْ أن تبتلع غصةً في صدرها. كان وقع كلماتها على أذني أقوى من أزيز المُسيَّرة الإسرائيلية في الخلفية، وقد تداخل معه بكاء الطفل الذي اهتزّ له الكون.

استطعتُ أخيراً الاتصال بهويدة، وهي ناشطة تعمل في إحدى المؤسسات التي تقدم دعماً من هذا النوع، بعدما تمكّنتُ من العثور على نقطة إرسال في موبايلي الذي دام انقطاعه أسبوعاً.

- مرحباً هويدة! كيف حالك؟ طمنيني عليكِ!

- الحمد لله بخير! هينا لهلقيت عايشين، وبنعارك في الحياة، زي ما انتَ شايف، كل شيء صعب.

- بِعين الله! بس أنا رنّيت عليكِ عشان موضوع مهم وبعرف أنك قدها، بدي بامبرز ضروري.

- الكميات محدودة، بس بدنا نحاول نضيف اسم الطفل وإن شاء الله خير، بكرة الصبح مُر عليّا، ما تقلق.

تحولت حياتي في زمن الإبادة إلى معارك مريرة متواصلة لتأمين متطلَّبات الحياة الأساسية والهرب من الموت من مكان لمكان. اكتسبتُ عادةً جديدة خلافاً لعادتي السابقة، إذ أصبحتُ أكثر استعجالاً للخروج من المنزل، حتى إن كلَّ من حولي لاحظوا همَّتي العالية بالمغادرة مبكراً، مبدين استغرابهم، كما لو أنني كنتُ أتعجّلُ موتي.

زوجتي أمل لم تكن تريدني أن أغادر البيت. كان الوقت يشارف الثامنة صباحاً. توسَّلت إليَّ كي أتأخَّر ساعة أو ساعتين، على الأقل، إلى أن يخرج الناس إلى الشوارع، معتقدةً أنَّ ذلك هو الوقت الآمن الذي تتراجع فيه وتيرة قصف المنازل والطرقات والبشر. كانت تحاول أنْ تدغدغ مشاعري بنظرات حنونة علَّها تستميلُ عواطفي فتنجح في مرادها؛ فهي تعلم جيداً أنني لا أرفض لها طلباً. وعندما لم تُجدِ هذه الطريقة نفعاً، لجأت إلى حيلة أخرى؛ إذ تظاهرت بالتعب، مدعيةً أنها تحتاجني بجوارها. وحين استنفدت جميع محاولاتها، طمأنتُها بأنني أريد أن أتفقّد أمي النازحة في منزل أختي، فأيقنتْ عندها أنَّ زيارتي لأمي سوف تستغرق ساعتين على الأقل، ليتحقّقَ لها ما تريد فعلياً، وهو الخروج لقضاء مهامي بعد العاشرة صباحاً.

ودّعتني وأوصتني بأنْ أتوخّى الحذر في الطريق، وأن أسلك الشوارع المكتظة، ظنّاً منها أنني سأكون أكثر أماناً وسط الناس، كأنها كانت تحاول أن تقنع نفسها أكثر مما تقنعني.

خلال مراحل النزوح المتعدِّدة، كثير من الأشياء التي طرأت على حياتي غيَّرتني. أصبحتُ بيتوتياً، أهتم بتحسين تفاصيل النزوح لأستطيع الصمود أكثر. بِتُّ أخاف أكثر. لم يكن هذا العدوان الإسرائيلي كسابقاته. إنه إبادة وعقاب جماعي. حين أسير في الشوارع، أرى وجوه شعبي الممحوّة الملامح، وأشعر بجيوبهم الخاوية عند كل بسطة أمُرُّ عليها. جميعُنا سواسية الآن؛ فرؤيتك لأحدهم والتمعُّن في تفاصيل ملابسه يجعلك تعرف ما حلَّ به، وكيف نخرته حرب الإبادة هذه، كما يجعلك تعرف كيف نخرتك أنت أيضاً.

كانت الساعة الثامنة والثلث حين طرقتُ باب بيت أختي نهاد. "شو الدعوة جاي بدري؟ يا ساتر، شو فيه؟ مالك؟ صاير إشي؟" طرحت عليَّ أسئلة متتابعة، ولم أكن قد خلعتُ حذائي بعد. اعترت وجهها ملامح الخوف والدهشة، كأنها كانت تنتظر مني أنْ أخبرها أنَّ أحد أفراد العائلة أصيب أو استشهد، أو أن أحد بيوت إخوتي طالته الصواريخ فسُوِّي بالأرض. في أوقات كهذه، لا أحد ينتظر أحداً يحمل خبراً مفرحاً. بل إنَّ الأخبار التي تأتي باكراً، في ظل هذه الإبادة المتواصلة، هي الأسوأ حتماً.

شعور بالسعادة غمرني حين رأيتُ البهجة على وجه أمي. لك أن تتخيَّل اللهفةَ في عينيّ أمٍّ التقت ولدها، بعدما تاه طويلاً. كادت أضلعي تتكسَّر من عناقها لي. اشتقتُ لأمي كثيراً، واشتقتُ لها أكثر وهي تتحسَّسُ بيديها ملامح وجهي. ابتسمت حتى تشنَّجت عضلات وجهها. ورغم هذه المشاعر الرقيقة، إلا أنَّ خوفها كان جلياً في نظراتها إليَّ، وقد طرحت عيناها أسئلة كثيرة. ودون أن تهمس لي بسؤال، أجبتُها بأنني مضطر للخروج باكراً كي أؤمِّن الحفاضات لطفل لجأت إليَّ أمُّه كي أوفرها لها، فهي نازحة مع أسرتها في خيمة في خان يونس، بعدما اضطروا إلى مغادرة بيتهم في الشمال، ولم يحملوا معهم سوى القليل من المتاع والملابس درءاً للبرد. زوجها كان يعمل بأجرة يومية، وقد فقد مصدر رزقه، وبالكاد يستطيع توفير قوت يومهم. لا يهم إن أكلا أو لا، كلُّ ما يعنيهما هو ألا ينقطع طفلهما من الحفاضات. حاولتُ أن أستعطف أمي بالحديث عن هذه السيدة وعائلتها، فأنا أعرفُ أمي جيداً، إذ كانت تستسلم عندما تستمع لمثل هذه الحالات، بل وتشجِّعني أكثر على خدمة المحتاجين، بشرط ألا أُعرِّض حياتي للخطر. ألحَّت عليَّ بأن أشرب الشاي وأتناول الدُّقة والبندورة، اتّقاءً للصداع. كانت تشعر بكل ما يدور في خلجات صدري من دون أن أبوح بكلمة، وتلبّي لي مرادي من دون أن أطلب، كأن عقلي وقلبي في كيان أمي.

كانت زيارتي لأمي قصيرة جداً، وهو أمر لم تعتَدْهُ مني، إذ كنتُ أخصّص لها ساعات. تحدثنا عن كل شيء في دقائق معدودة. أردتُ الانطلاق إلى وجهتي لعلّي أحظى بشيء من فرح العائلة بتوفير الحفاضات.

بدأت أمي توجِّه لي النصائح بعدما شرحتُ لها أهمية الانطلاق باكراً. وصيَّتها لي: "لا تدخل من هذا الشارع، فيه بيت مهدَّد بالقصف، ادخُل من الشارع الثاني!"، وأشارت بيدها باتجاه شارع لا يؤدي لوجهتي، فأدركتُ بأنه اختلطت عليها الاتجاهات. على عَجل، انتعلتُ حذائي بالقرب من الباب، وشربتُ الشاي الذي صبَّته لي أمي في كوب ورقي، في رشفاتٍ متسارعة.

كان وجه أمي المشحون بالخوف يرافقني في الطريق، كظل راعش.

ماذا لو قُصف الشارع الذي أمشي فيه؟

توقفت. حاولتُ أنْ أستعيد وصية أمي، محاولاً أن أتبيَّن "الشارع الثاني" الذي أشارت إليه.

ماذا لو ضللتُ الطريق؟

تخيَّلتُ أمي منهارة، وأمل تبكي. سرَّعتُ خطوي. لكن الأسئلة لاحقتني، بإلحاح ينذر بالشؤم.

أمل التي أعهدُ إليها في كل مرة بوصية ترفض سماعها، تُجادلني ثم تبكي، هل ستنفِّذها؟

كيف سيكون شكل الزعل والحزن؟

كيف سيكون طفلي حمزة عندما يكبر؟

كيف ستكون حياته؟

هل سيتذكر شيئاً منّي أو عنّي؟

هل ستبقى في ذاكرته لحظات الأب والابن، وتلك المرات التي غفرتُ له فيها شقاوته، يشفع له فيها ذكاؤه وخفَّة دمّه؟

ثم لاحَ أمامي سؤال مرعب، حاولتُ أن أكمِّمه: هل سيكبر حمزة؟

في تلك اللحظة، سقطت كلُّ الأسئلة والخواطر المرعبة من رأسي أمام رعب أعظم انقضَّ عليَّ من سماء غزة التي تمطر موتاً. سقط صاروخ. دويُّ انفجاره تخطى وحدات قياس الصوت، وارتطامه بالأرض رجَّ كياني، ومزَّق صور أمي وأمل وحمزة التي كانت تتزاحم في رأسي.

اصطدمتُ بمنظر شاب سقط أمامي، لأجدَ نفسي في صراع بين رغبتي الغريزية في النجاة ونزعتي الإنسانية بحمله وإسعافه. تغلَّبت فطرتي بالهروب والنجاة بروحي، وما إن استدرتُ بحثاً عن حائط أحتمي به، حتى سقط الصاروخ الثاني، بعد أقل من دقيقة على سقوط الصاروخ الأول. رفعني الصاروخ وقذفني مسافة أربعة أمتار. تمزَّقت ثيابي، وأصيبت ساقاي بحروق، فيما امتلأ حذائي بالدم. لكنني، أرغمتُ نفسي على متابعة السير، أعرُج ملتمساً الأمان. فكرة واحدة استحوذت عليّ لحظتها، أكثر مما كنتُ أفكِّر بجراحي: أمي، لقد سمعتْ الانفجار.

تجاهلتُ الألم، وجررْتُ نفسي إلى بيت نهاد؛ أنفاسي متقطِّعة، ورؤيتي مشوَّشة، وشعري ووجهي يكسوهما الغبار. كان بنطلوني ممزَّقاً، وقدمي غارقة في الدم.

أخيراً وصلتُ الباب. وكنتُ أستطيع أن أسمع صوتها يقطر ألماً، يتخلَّله بكاء يعتصر القلب. "عبد الله! عبد الله!"، كانت أمي تنادي عليّ بصوت متهدِّج، تغلَّف بالذعر.

استجمعتُ ما تبقى لدي من قوة، وفتحتُ الباب. رفعتُ ذراعيّ، ودرتُ حول نفسي ببطء لأطمئنها بأنني بخير. مشيتُ بضع خطوات أتَّكئ على كبريائي، وأنا أشعر بألم شديد في قدمي وبطني.

أردتُ جداً أن أنهار بين ذراعي أمي وأبكي كطفل. لكنني لم أستطع. حبستُ دموعي، وكتمتُ خوفي، واخترتُ الصمت.

لا أعلم إلى متى سأبقى صامتاً.

من خيمة إلى خيمة

لبنى مقداد

في اليوم السابع والستين من الاجتياح الإسرائيلي، نزحنا من بيت العائلة في مدينة حمد إلى أرض زراعية في مواصي خان يونس، نبتت فيها العشرات من خيام النزوح. مكثنا في خيمة قام أفراد من عائلتنا الممتدة، من بينهم خالي وأبناؤه، ببنائها من النايلون الأبيض والخشب. كانت مؤلَّفة من شقّين؛ شقّ رجالي فيه سجادة قديمة متهالكة للنوم، وطاولة خشبية عليها أدوات المطبخ، وبجانبها موقد غاز، وتحت الطاولة بعض معلبّات الطعام التي كنا نضطرُّ إلى شرائها، رغم أنه من المفترض أن تُوزَّع مجّاناً ضمن حزم المساعدات الغذائية على النازحين أمثالنا؛ وشقّ نسائي ننام فيه على الحصيرة، وفيه بعض البطانيات، وبعض أكياس الطحين التي اشتريناها بثمن خيالي بعد مرور شهرين من الحصار الإسرائيلي، دون أن تتوفر حفنة طحين. وبين الشقّين بطانية قديمة مدعوكة، تفصلُ الرجال عن النساء.

في الجهة الخلفية من الخيمة، كان هناك حائط يُطوِّق الأرض الزراعية، وضعنا عليه بعض المقتنيات التي جلبناها معنا من بيتنا، الذي استحال بيت الذكريات. كنّا، نحن النساء، نتشارك في الفراش مع الصغار لنتدفّأ. وسادتي كانت عبارة عن معطف أرتديه حيثما أذهب، قبل أنْ يصبح له استخدام مزدوج. أصابعي مشقَّقة من شدَّة البرد، ويداي محروقتان ومتعبتان من نزوح إجباري، ورأسي مُتصدِّع من طنين "زنّانة" في السماء، حتى إذا ارتميتُ آخر اليوم على الحصيرة، ظللتُ أتأمل ما حلَّ بي وبمدينتي وبحياتي.

خان يونس، المدينة الجميلة كعروس دائمة البهاء، أصبحت أنقاضاً، رويداً رويداً. كل يوم، كنتُ أرى مبانيَ سكنيةً تجلس كالقوقعة مطبقة بعضها فوق بعض، وأبراجاً تحولت إلى جبال من الركام، وشوارع فرغت من جوفها. وبين خيمةٍ وأخرى حكايات لم تنتهِ، وحياة تمضي نحو حتفها، وذكريات يصنعها الألم.

ذات ليلة، وفي تمام الساعة السابعة مساءً، هطلت الصواريخ من صوب البحر والبر والجو. لم نكن نعلم ماذا كان يدور خارج خيمتنا، وأين سقطت الصواريخ. الاتصال بالأقارب في أماكن النزوح الأخرى لم يكن بالأمر السهل. معظم الوقت، كنا نعرف ما يجري من خلال ما تتناقله القنوات الإخبارية. لكن بات من الصعب تتبُّع الأحداث، بسبب الانقطاع شبه الدائم في الكهرباء منذ الساعات الأولى للعدوان. تجمَّدنا في مكاننا من الصدمة، لا ندري ماذا نفعل، ننتظر أن تتَّضح الصورة، فيما تصاعدت ألسنة النيران المستعرة في المنطقة التي سقطت فيها الصواريخ، وقد امتلأت الأجواء برائحة الفسفور الأبيض، فاختنقت أنفاسُنا.

داهم جيش الاحتلال منطقتنا، من دون أن يُخطرنا بإخلائها. دخلت الدبّابات والجرّافات الإسرائيلية من أعلى التلة المعروفة باسم "المحرَّرات". تقدَّمت آليات الاحتلال إلى الأرض التي كانت تؤوينا. صوَّبت الدبابات قذائفها على الناس المختبئين في خيمهم، في حين تقدَّمت نحو البوابة التي تفتح على الأرض الزراعية مدرَّعة محمَّلة بالجنود كانت ترفع علماً أصفر. سمعنا الصواريخ تصفِّر من كل اتجاه، كما كان أزيز الرصاص والقذائف يخترق الهواء مراراً وتكراراً. وعلى الرغم من الخوف والقلق، إلا أننا قُمنا، أنا وابن خالي الذي يصغرني ببضع سنوات، بطهو الطعام المكون من لحم معلَّبات اللانشون التي كنا نعاف أن نأكلها في بيوتنا في زمن السلم الغابر، ومعه الفلفل الحلو والبصل وبعض البهارات. قلَّبنا الطعام على نار هادئة، ثم سكبناه في صحن أبيض عريض، وقدَّمناه مع بعض الزيتون الأخضر. كان الطعام لذيذاً، رغم تقشُّفه وبساطة مكوناته.

أردنا أن نأكل كلَّ شيء معاً، لأن الدبابات اقتربت منا، وبعدها كان يمكن أن نرحل إلى الله في أي وقت.

اشتدَّ إطلاق القذائف. قرَّرنا أن نشرب النسكافيه، كعادة آثرنا ألا نتخلّى عنها، رغم انقطاعه مدة طويلة بسبب إغلاق المعابر. وزَّعنا مع أكواب النسكافيه جميع أنواع البسكويت التي اضطُررنا لشرائها، إذ اشتهيناها في زمن الحرب، مع أنها هي الأخرى كانت من بين المساعدات الغذائية التي تُوزَّع على شعبنا الجائع في غزة مجاناً.

في الساعة التاسعة مساء، بدأ صوت هدير الدبابات الإسرائيلية يشتدُّ مع تقدُّمها، ونحن نضحك ونمزح معاً. كان بعض أفراد العائلة متفاجئين من حرصنا على إعداد العشاء وشهيَّتنا المفتوحة على النسكافيه والبسكويت وسط زحف الجيش

الإسرائيلي نحونا. وما فاجأهم أكثر هو ضحكنا بشكل هستيري، نحن الذين أُرغمنا على النزوح من بيتنا، الذي كان مرجَّحاً جداً أن نموت تحت أنقاضه، إلى مكان اعتقدنا بأنه آمن.

تنامى إلينا صوت صراخ: "إسعاف.. إسعاف!". كان جارنا أبو بسام، الكائن منزله بمحاذاة الأرض الزراعية. اخترقت قذيفة دبابة حائط الغرفة التي كان يجلس فيها، فطالته الشظايا هو وأبناؤه. لكنّنا كنّا عاجزين عن مساعدتهم. لم نعرف ما حلَّ به وبأسرته. لم نعد نسمع نداءاته. تساءلنا ما إذا كان أحد الجيران تمكَّن من إنقاذهم. من ناحيتنا، كانت القذائف الإسرائيلية تمطر في كل مكان من حولنا بغزارة. كان من شبه المستحيل مغادرة الأرض الزراعية، لأن المدرَّعة الإسرائيلية، بالعلم الأصفر الذي كان يعدنا بمزيد من القتل، أصبحت قريبة جداً من البوابة. تَتابَع إطلاق القذائف، تلفُّ ليلَنا بلونها الأحمر النازف. لم نتوقع أن ننجو، لكننا نجونا بمعجزة إلهية.

في فلق الصباح، نظرنا من الثقوب التي أحدثتها القذائف في البوابة، فلم نرَ الدبابات والجرافات الإسرائيلية أمامنا. خرج خالي من البوابة لرؤية من بقي حولنا من الناس، فوجد رجلاً مسنّاً يرتدي جلابيةً بيضاء. وجهه الملتحي شاحب اللون، تلبَّسته علامات الخوف والرعب من أن يقتنصه جندي أو يُقتل برصاصة من "الكواد كابتر" التي لم تتوقف عن إطلاق النار. كان المسنُّ قد غادر المنطقة حين دخلها الجنود الإسرائيليون، وقد عاد إليها ليأخذ بعض أغراضه، محذِّراً من وجود دبابة إسرائيلية مدفونة فوق التلة العالية، للمراقبة، وأن باقي الدبابات تقدَّمت نحو مستشفى الخير، في المواصي. أخبرنا بأنه يتعين علينا مغادرة المكان بسرعة. توتَّرت أعصابنا بعد هذه الكلمات. في البداية، خفنا أن نمشي خوفاً من الطائرة المسيَّرة التي كانت تصوب نحو أي شخص يتحرك. لكن، كان يجب أن نغادر المنطقة.

حملنا حقائبنا وأمتعتنا، وخرجنا على دفعات، بحيث إذا لم تنجُ المجموعة الأولى، تستطيع الثانية انتشال أشلائنا بعد موتنا. هذا ما فكَّرنا فيه.

خرجتُ أنا وأخواتي وبنات العائلة نسير بحذر بين الأزقة في المنطقة، قبل أن تتبعنا بعد وقت كافٍ، بما ضمن نجاتنا على الأقل حتى حينه، المجموعةُ الثانية.

كانت الخيام والبيوت المجاورة قد أتت عليها النيران. رأيتُ الحُفر الغائرة التي خلّفتها القذائف التي ضربت بيت أبو بسام. وحين سألتُ عنه لاحقاً، أخبرني أحد المارة بأنه نُقل مع أبنائه إلى مستشفى أبو يوسف النجار في رفح.

علت الدهشة وجوه الناس وهم يتابعوننا بنظراتهم. كانوا متفاجئين، أو بالأحرى غير مصدقين، بأننا ما زلنا على قيد الحياة، رغم ما تعرّضنا له في الليلة السابقة من قصفٍ متواصل للدبابات الإسرائيلية وتغولّها في منطقتنا. قطعنا أكثر من خمسة كيلومترات مشياً على الأقدام. كان هناك تزاحم في الطريق بين المشاة والشاحنات التي كانت تنقل الناس من منطقة خان يونس إلى رفح، هاربين إلى أماكن يعتقدون أنها أكثر أمناً.

من شدة التزاحم افترقنا، شقيقتي وأنا، عن باقي العائلة. قررنا أن نتابع المسير إلى منطقة الشاكوش، في مواصي رفح، التي خبّرنا خالي عنها، على أمل أن نلتقي جميعاً فيها. وبعد تعب المشي والتلفّت خلفنا طوال الوقت، جلسنا بين النازحين الآخرين على تلّة عالية نراقب المارة، نحاول الاتصال بأيٍّ من إخوتي أو أحد أفراد العائلة، دون جدوى.

أخيراً، بعد هبوط الليل، تمكنّا من الاتصال بهم، والتقينا جميعاً. شيّدنا خيمةً جديدة، ونمنا متلاصقين، فإذا سقطَ الموت علينا رحلنا معاً، وإذا أبقت علينا الحياة، عشنا معاً.

شكر وتقدير

هذا العمل الأدبي الذي يضم أصواتاً شابة من غزة خلال الإبادة الجماعية التي بدأت في الثامن من أكتوبر 2023، هو ثمرة جهد شارك فيه كثيرون بحب وإخلاص. كانت هناك نسخة أولى مبكرة من الأنطولوجيا كان من المقرّر أن تصدر عن "دار فلسطين تكتب" للنشر تحت مظلة مهرجان "فلسطين تكتب"، حيث نتوجّه بالشكر إلى كلٍّ من: سوزان معوّض درّاج، وإيمان غنيم، و إبراهيم العزّة، وزاهي خميس، على جهودهم في تلك النسخة. كما نتوجّه بشكر خاص لحمادة القبط، الرسام الغزّي الذي يزين عمله الفني المدهش غلاف هذا الكتاب.

لكننا انتقلنا إلى مسار آخر حين تلقّينا عرضاً من دار "سايمون أند شوستر"، حيث قامت حزامة حبايب بتحرير شامل ومعمَّق للنصوص باللغة العربية، وأُعيدت ترجمة النسخة الإنجليزية بالكامل.

نتقدّم بخالص الامتنان إلى رولا حرب وأليساندرا باستاغلي في "وان سيغنال" لاضطلاعهما بمتابعة نشر هذه الأنطولوجيا، وإلى كل العاملين في "سايمون أند شوستر" الذين أسهموا في إخراج هذا الكتاب إلى النور ووصوله إلى القرّاء؛ كما نخصُّ بالشكر أنجالي سينغ، من وكالة أنجالي سينغ، لجهودها في الترويج لهذا المشروع ودعمه منذ البداية.

جاءت هذه الأصوات كما هي، خام وأصيلة، دون أن تخضع لفلترة أو رقابة أو إقصاء من أي نوع. وخلال الأشهر التي شهدت العدوان الإسرائيلي الوحشي على غزّة، وجّه العديد من الناس انتقادات في محلّها لوسائل الإعلام الغربية التي عمدت إلى ترديد روايات زائفة، وامتناعها عن تسمية الإبادة باسمها وتسليط الضوء عليها، وفشلها في طرح الأسئلة الصعبة على الساسة، وتعمّدها تغييب وجهة النظر الفلسطينية.

تأسست "دار فلسطين تكتب" بوصفها ذراع النشر لمهرجان "فلسطين تكتب"، وهي مؤسسة تجمع العاملين في الثقافة الفلسطينية حول العالم؛ فيما تمارس "جمعية الثقافة والفكر الحر" في غزة دورها في احتضان الروح الفلسطينية المبدعة بكل ما يتاح لها من سُبل.

وانسجاماً مع رسالة هاتين المؤسستين، نعتز بأن نجمع هذه الأصوات المهمّة لفلسطينيين عاشوا - وما زالوا يعيشون – أهوال محرقة مستمرة.